LARRY ROCQUIN

IF ONLY GOD...

HOW DESPERATION LED
TO THE SUPERNATURAL

If Only God…

How Desperation Led to the Supernatural

Copyright © 2020 by Larry Rocquin

Cover design and Author photo by Victoria Rocquin

Unless otherwise noted, scripture quotations are from the New King James Version of the Bible.

ISBN-13: 978-1-7336624-7-5

Printed in the United States of America

2020 – First Edition

Published by

CHRISTIAN DAY Publishing Co. ™

6148 Jones Road, Flowery Branch, GA 30542

DEDICATION

This book is dedicated to my wife and best friend Rinalda, better known as "Wonder Woman" in our family.

Throughout our thirty-four years of marriage, her adventurous spirit and selflessness enabled us to go literally anywhere that God has led us around the world.

They say she can make dinner "out of thin air" and I believe it may be true.

This book is also dedicated to all who are cut from a different mold. You are the ones who are desperately seeking more of God.

You are the ones who are not satisfied in attending church once a week and checking that off your list.

You are the ones who are not interested in discussing doctrines or past revivals; you want to be at ground zero, where revival is happening right now!

You are the ones who could be labeled "desperadoes for God."

You are the few that are desperate for His presence!

SPECIAL THANKS

The revival mentioned in this book might have happened in a different city or a different church, but it didn't.

Because of the people I'm about to mention, God poured out His Spirit in Paulina, and the Southeast Louisiana Revival was born.

To the Southeast Louisiana Revival Pastors - Jeff McKneely, Donnie Shaffer, Mervin Strother, and Sonny Wahl - I express my heart-felt thanks for taking the leap of faith with me to see God pour out His Spirit and bring revival to Louisiana.

To Pastors Jerry and Sandi Claunch, my father and mother in the Lord, and my first pastors: Thank you for believing in me when few did. You gave me every opportunity to minister.

Thanks to Maurice and Myrna Jordan, who believed in me and encouraged me, and also, to Sandra Bailey Simmons, who not only believed in me, but invested countless hours into my life.

To my present pastors, Dr. Michael and Sister Elaine Mille': You have poured so much into my life for the past twenty-plus years, and, if not for you, I might not still be in the ministry.

Thanks to all the men I won't mention by name, but who stood with me through seven years of prayer, and refused to give up until "God showed up." And He did!

Thanks to Anthony Marquise who has been a faithful friend and sounding board throughout our ministry.

Thanks to Daniel and Valerie Millet, who helped pioneer the Paulina church and who were here when we arrived twenty years ago. You have faithfully served the Lord through thick and thin. You have - at many times and in countless ways - encouraged us in our darkest hours. Valerie was also the initial editor of this book. Thanks also to Daron Hannan, who edited for us in the midnight hour.

Thanks to our daughter Victoria, who has worked tirelessly at all of our revivals, and on this book.

Lastly, I want to express a special thanks to my "Woodville buddies," Patric Herbert and Jebby Baldwin, who always believed in me. Without you men, this work may never have been penned.

God has used all our relationships and their interactions in our lives to bring us to the place we are today.

Someone once said, "If you see a turtle sitting on the top of a fencepost, he didn't get there by himself!"

Thank you, my brothers and sisters! May God richly bless you.

ENDORSEMENTS

Dr. Jesse Duplantis

So many people live in the excuse of "If Only…" all their lives, only to come to the end and feel full of regret for "what *could* have been." In this compelling book, Pastor Larry Rocquin will inspire you to push past limitations, regrets, and "if only's" in your life once and for all. I encourage you to get this book. It's a revelation of what seeking God and coming together in the unity of the faith can do – in a life, in a church, in a city, in a state, in a nation. I believe you will enjoy this book just like I did.

Dr. Jesse Duplantis
Jesse Duplantis Ministries

Pastor Todd Smith

The first time I met Pastor Larry was at the North Georgia Revival in Dawsonville, Georgia. I was briefly introduced to him minutes before the start of our Sunday morning service. In my heart I knew there was something different about him and his wife.

Spiritual hunger is a beautiful thing and to say God is attracted to it is an epic understatement. God is relentless and will move Heaven and earth to encounter someone desperate for Him.

Pastor Larry and his wife Rinalda drove over eight hours to Dawsonville from Paulina, Louisiana, because they heard that God's glory was present at Christ Fellowship Church. They came because they desired an authentic move of God in their lives and church.

God did not disappoint. The two of them encountered the fire and glory of God at the altar, as well as in the baptismal waters of the North Georgia Revival. I must say again, the fire of God hit them both. Not only was his physical body miraculously healed, but his heart and ministry were changed.

This book vividly tells that remarkable story and their current journey of revival.

In this book, *"If Only God...How Desperation Led to the Supernatural,"* Larry Rocquin hits the bullseye.

It's not every day that you read a book that captures your mind, heart and interest from the very beginning and keeps it all the way through, this is such a book.

Pastor Larry chronicles his journey with vivid imagery and captivating stories. I loved the stories! Each page pulls you closer to the people he writes about and to the God that met him in the water.

Today, because of his testimony and pursuit of God, Southeast Louisiana is engulfed in revival fire.

As you read this book the same will happen to you.

Be prepared for your hunger and desperation for God to go to the next level.

Blessings,

Todd Smith, Christ Fellowship Church, Dawsonville, GA, NORTH GEORGIA REVIVAL

Pastor Jerry Claunch

If you are hungry for a down-to-earth, honest look into the miraculous workings of the Holy Spirit in this day of doubt, fear and uncertainty, this book by Pastor Larry Rocquin is for you!

Pastor Rocquin tells it like he sees it, and the way he has personally experienced it.

"Seen and experienced" *what*, you ask?

The miraculous supernatural moving of the Holy Spirit setting folks free, healing sickness and disease as well as restoring and reconciling broken relationships that have defied the great efforts of much counseling, medication and medical treatments.

As I read "*If Only God*" for the first time, I experienced the stirrings of the Holy Spirit that encouraged, strengthened, and deepened my desire for the real and genuine presence of God that ushers in the miraculous and supernatural. A huge shout-out to Pastor Larry for this wonderful and very personal account of the moving of the

Holy Spirit TODAY!

Jerry Claunch, Masters of Theology, New Orleans Baptist Theology Seminary

Executive Pastor, Eagle Heights Church of Memphis, Memphis, TN

Founding Pastor, Church of Faith, Hammond, LA

Dr. Jerry King

A couple of days ago, I was asked to read and assess an about-to-be-published document by Pastor Larry Rocquin.

I could not put it down once I started to read it. The passion of pursuit of God, even in the face of long periods of His seeming silence, obviously did not prevent prolonged periods of determined praise and prayer - pursuit of unity, with other pastors who agreed with him to combine their effort and not let go before the result they sought was attained!

And when miracles began to occur, the determined fervor was not dimmed.

I believe the church needs this book to help inspire more of us to pay the price for revival our God desires more fervently than we could ever match!

I congratulate Pastor Rocquin on his preparation, and for making this tool valuable to us all.

Jerry A. King, ThD

FOREWORD

It is with great excitement, honor and humility that I sit to write the foreword to this incredible book.

Larry and Rinalda Rocquin have been examples to me for 30 years - examples of what it means to follow Christ, to be a minister, a family man and friend.

They took me under their wings shortly after I was saved and taught me how to evangelize and love others. We did street ministry, prison ministry, nursing home ministry and small groups together as we desired to please Him, touch the lost and advance His Kingdom.

I was amazed that Larry wanted me - a freshly saved twenty-one-year-old kid with a horrible past, who was still covered in the dust of the world - to help him in ministry.

I'm forever grateful!

In 1992, Larry and Rinalda heard the call to move to the former Soviet Union as church planting missionaries. Six months later, I arrived in Russia on a cold November day to be the youth pastor of the church they had just planted in Furmanov, Russia.

I just took you on a brief stroll down memory lane because I know Larry, possibly like few others. We have spent years together; I have lived with him and Rinalda, shared countless meals, and "survived" numerous, crazy cross-cultural ministry situations.

Larry is the real deal! In over thirty years, I have never seen his love for God fade one bit: neither his desire to know God more, nor his passion for ministry.

In this book, you will be taken on a journey, seeing what happens when people get desperate for a touch from God. You will read how an unusual revival was birthed in an unexpected place. You will read of many miracles, conversions, baptisms in the Holy Spirit and recommitments to Christ.

I have been blessed to be a part of this revival from the beginning. I was there to see many of the miracles you will read about. I personally know the people and can testify to the work of grace in their lives.

You are about to read the account of something that happened, not hundreds of years ago, but recently - in our time.

Not only did it happen, but it is still happening, and is continuing to spread and touch others all around the world.

I pray that, as you read the chapters in this book, you will experience God in a new way.

I pray that you will see that miracles, revival and Kingdom living are in reach, and *normal* for every believer.

May your expectation of what God can and will do in your life, family, and ministry grow as you journey through the pages of this book.

"If only God..."

Pastor Mervin Strother, Cornerstone Church, Amite LA

INTRODUCTION

Inside every person is a hope that God exists and really cares.

You can go through life "doing your own thing," but when you come face to face with the very real presence of God, when you witness first-hand a real miracle that cannot be explained, when the presence of God touches your very being, it is a life-altering experience.

In my personal quest for God I have come across a truly wonderful discovery! I have experienced the presence of God in an unmistakably tangible way. I have come to the realization that He can change the things medicine cannot cure, and years of counseling will not fix. Yes! God can, and does, heal and deliver!

Some people think, "If only I knew that God was there; If only I knew that God was listening; and If only I knew that God really cared about me." There are many who are angry with God. They go through life dwelling on how God has failed them in some way and let them down.

Still others claim to have spoken to God, but their unanswered prayers lead them to question, "Where was God when I needed Him?" These are questions that people have asked throughout the ages, but the answers are not found in asking the same old questions over and over. The answer is found simply when our personal relationship with God becomes renewed and revived. That is when answers that were already there become clearer.

People's interactions with God are very individualized. Like thumbprints, no two are alike. We all have our own childhood upbringing, cultural differences and life experiences. Just as our relationships with different people are unique, so will our individual relationship with God be unique.

You are about to discover for yourself that there is a real God who wants to have a real relationship with you. He really does care for you and He doesn't have favorites. If you already have a relationship with Him, what you are about to read will challenge you to develop a deeper relationship with God.

This book is a first-hand account of how a small group of believers pressed in diligently over a period of time, and how that perseverance resulted in a phenomenal encounter with the living God. When God showed up in power, it changed the lives of everyone who encountered Him, many of whose testimonies are inserted into the narrative of this book.

All of the miracles recounted in this book were witnessed by numerous people who, to this day, feel humbled and honored to have seen God at work.

I believe the essence of this book was placed on my heart because of you. Its purpose, therefore, is to encourage you, whoever you are.

You may be recently devastated by divorce, or a teenager struggling to discover who you really are, or someone battling a debilitating diagnosis.

Whoever you are, this book is for you. You are very special to God.

You may be in a battle with alcohol or drugs, or you may be one living in uncertainty about the future. This book is for you, because God cares for you.

You may be a pastor shepherding a small congregation on the backside of nowhere, or a layperson who has been faithfully serving God for years, yet unsatisfied with where you are in life or with God. This book is for you.

Basically, I am speaking to anyone who is in a place where he or she recognizes a desperate need for God. If you have found yourself described in these paragraphs, be encouraged. This book is for YOU. Because God loves YOU.

Let's get started on a journey into the supernatural!

TABLE OF CONTENTS

Chapter 1

The Day God Shook the Church

From the time I was a child I was taught that if you wanted to hear from God, you would have to pray.

As the new pastor of St. James Community Church in Paulina, Louisiana, I knew that from the look of things, we needed a lot of prayer! I knew what most pastors know: that the hardest thing to get people to show up for is prayer.

At the Great Commission Fellowship Conference in 2015, my pastor, Dr. Michael Mille, asked, "What would happen if some of you pastors bit some carpet early in the morning?"

I knew exactly what he meant, and that statement haunted me because, as much as I knew that I needed a move of God, I wondered if I was really willing to pay the price.

Well, I have heard it said that a man will do anything if he's desperate enough. And I was desperate for the presence of God!

For one year, I got up before dawn and worshiped God on my keyboard. Alone in my room, I worshiped for what turned out to be five-, six-, and ten-hour sessions. I probably clocked 1300 to 1400 hours of worship in that one year alone, focusing on songs about the Holy Spirit. When I tell this story, people always say something like this, "Man, I bet that the presence of God was thick in that place."

The surprising thing is, it wasn't, and I always replied with something along these lines, "No, it was as dead as a doorknob."

I believe that my perseverance during that year of worship was a major key to what was about to take place. Unknown to me, we were about to see a great outpouring of God's Spirit unlike anything any of us had ever witnessed.

We were in our seventh year of a weekly men's prayer meeting that always began by making a list of prayer needs. We would faithfully ask the Holy Spirit to move in our church, and we'd start with a couple of worship songs; then, one by one, the men would come to the microphone and pray.

"What would happen if some of you pastors bit some carpet early in the morning?"
Dr. Michael Mille

In August of 2016, our men's prayer meeting was closing with a couple of worship songs. I asked the men to raise their hands and receive more of the Holy Spirit.

Unaware that anything had happened, I asked if anyone wanted personal prayer. One of the older men asked for prayer for pain in his feet, and we prayed for him. Then as I was about to pray for the next young man, he said, "I have one question. What the heck is going on around here?"

I was confused and asked him to explain. He said, "Something came through the ceiling and hit me, ran through my body, and went into the floor. Besides that," he said, "all the hair on my body is standing on end. I want to know, what the heck was that?"

The older man said, "Son, that's what we are here for!"

The young man responded, "Well, if that's what we are looking for, it's here!"

That's when it all started.

At the following Thursday night prayer group, we experienced another supernatural move of the Spirit. The presence of God was so thick and weighty that it seemed like one could cut it with a knife.

In the Old Testament the Hebrew word for glory is "*Kabod*," which has a primitive root meaning "heavy." This doesn't mean heavy in the sense of being a burden, but heavy in the positive sense, like the power of His glory and honor, presence and majesty.

At our very next prayer meeting, after the second worship song, one of the young men looked like a deer caught in a headlight, and most of the men couldn't move; they looked as if they were frozen in time. One of the men managed to make it to the microphone and started singing; another man was on his face crying out to God. There was a holy awe in the meeting. The presence of God was there!

We had come to expect His presence at our meetings, and sure enough, when the first note was played the following week at the men's meeting, God's Spirit moved mightily. Two of the men were approaching the microphone and were literally blown back about ten feet. A third man who was praying at a table said, "Whatever that was, it just went through me and the table, and down the hallway!"

Another man approached the microphone, and before speaking, quickly looked back and forth as if looking for someone. I asked him what he was doing and he said, "Somebody put his hand on my shoulder, but there's nobody there."

At once, he burst into tears and sat down, visibly shaken! One of the men felt that raindrops were falling from the ceiling. He said, "It felt so real that I thought there was a hole in the ceiling."

We wanted the movement of the Holy Spirit to take place in the main sanctuary on Sunday morning. It may sound foolish now, but at the time we weren't quite sure if God's presence would actually move with us into the main sanctuary building.

Sunday, September 4, 2016

Like any other Sunday morning, we gathered in our main sanctuary to begin the morning service. Some of the men from our prayer group asked to pray for the worship team. As the men prayed, some claimed the worship team had heat rising from their heads.

After worship, before I preached the morning message, I went to the piano and led the congregation in that old song, "Holy, Holy, Holy, Lord God Almighty." We sang this song many times in our men's prayer group, because it always seemed to usher in God's presence! Honestly, I thought that it would prime the pump and that God would move, but nothing happened.

When we were halfway through the morning message, I extended my hand toward the congregation and shouted, "Somebody shout 'Jesus!'"

At that moment the heavens thundered so loud that my wife, Rinalda, had to catch herself from falling off her seat! A few of the men ran outside to see if the building was damaged. I turned to look through the window and to my amazement there was not a cloud in the sky!

I continued preaching and I asked once again, "Could somebody shout 'Jesus'?"

The sound of thunder came again, so unexpectedly, that it took us all by surprise. We knew there was no way that anyone could make thunder clap at a precise moment, but it did.

I asked the people to shout "Jesus" once again, two more times. And yes, the thunder clapped violently again!

Curiously, I turned to look through the window again, and - you guessed it - there was not a cloud in the sky. That holy awe fell on the congregation as we witnessed the tangible presence of God.

"Could somebody shout 'Jesus'?"

There were also various Holy Spirit manifestations during the same service.

One man said, "It felt like waves that kept coming, then stopped, and when I surrendered a certain thing in my life, then the waves began again."

Another said, "It seemed like a warmth up near the platform area in church."

One husband said it felt like he and his wife were covered in warmth. Several people felt waves, and they said it felt like they were about to be knocked to the ground. Several of our members said they smelled wood burning. I was reminded of the Old Testament scripture in Leviticus 8:18-21, where it speaks of burnt offerings. Another person said there was the sweet smell of flowers; Jesus is known as the Rose of Sharon.

When the service ended, the men from our prayer meetings gathered with me near the platform, and we joined hands and prayed, "Lord, we have no idea what You are wanting to do here, but whatever it is, we want it!"

I honestly thought that on the next Sunday, every member of our church would invite everyone they knew and that we would have the next great revival!

My mind raced with thoughts of the great revivals of the early 1800s held by Charles Finney, when entire towns were saved and transformed by the power of God. That was not the case at all for us.

Over the next three Sunday services there was not one new person in church, but there were varied manifestations.

After that, there were no major movements in our Sunday morning services. However, in our Thursday night men's prayer meetings there continued to be a steady serving of the tangible presence of God.

There was no doubt that we had encountered the "heavy" glory of God's presence. I was certain of two things: first, we had no idea of what He wanted us to do; second, this didn't happen by accident, but because we were desperate for His presence.

Questions for Reflection:

1. Was there ever a time in your life that you experienced an encounter with God?
2. What precipitated that encounter?
3. How did it affect your life?

Chapter 2

God, Where Are You?

For the next two and a half years we never again experienced that "heavy" presence of God in our main sanctuary. We did continue to experience a strong presence in every one of our men's prayer and worship meetings. My question was, "God, where are you?"

Where We Came From

Many ministers can boast of being a third or fourth generation preacher. That is not the case for me. When I was radically saved at the age of twenty-nine, I was raised in a Christian family, but from what I remember, no one worked very hard at it. My wife, Rinalda, comes from a wonderful Baptist family; her father was a deacon in their church. The joke is that her whole family is Baptist, even the family cat!

Giving up Everything

For years, I had owned my own business, and Rinalda was a college instructor. We went to Bible college together and set our sights on doing something for the Lord. In 1990, the Iron Curtain fell, and by 1992 we had left everything behind and moved to Ivanova, Russia.

In the eight years we were there, we started three churches and two feeding centers. We purchased a barroom and a funeral home and renovated them into churches. We held thirty-three marriage seminars across Russia, all the way to Siberia, Mongolia, and even to Africa. We also gave oversight to nine churches. It seemed like anything we put our hands to prospered!

Bringing it All Back Home

When we returned to the United States, we were asked to hold a marriage seminar at a church in Paulina, Louisiana. The Lord made it plain to us that we were to pastor this church and put down roots.

The church had been through turmoil, and lost their pastor; there were a lot of broken people. With only 22,000 people in the whole parish, we were in the middle of nowhere, surrounded by sugarcane fields. This small farming community in Paulina is actually called Grand Point, where locals tell the story of its fertile soil deposited by the Mississippi River overflowing its banks long before any of them were born.

I also know the names of those who labored for the Lord here before me, so I know that spiritual "seeds" have been planted, and the fields are fertile in more than one way.

I know the Old Testament prophet wasn't speaking

about Grand Point when he wrote, "*Shepherd Your people with your scepter, the flock of Your possession which dwells by itself in the woodland, in the midst of a fruitful field...*" (Micah 7:14 NAS), but one of my church members points out the fact that our building is on a piece of land that was once a cane field, situated at the edge of wooded wetlands. And of course, Rinalda and I did find one of God's "flocks" there.

Since I know that "*the eyes of the Lord search the whole earth in order to strengthen those whose hearts are fully committed to Him...*" (2 Chronicles 16:9 NLV), Rinalda and I laid our hearts down in that "cane field," believing it was "white for harvest" (John 4:35 ESV), and confident that He would "strengthen" us through this work.

We renamed the church St. James Community Church after St. James Parish, which is where our church is located. (In Louisiana, when we talk about parishes, we are talking about counties.)

Needless to say, our ministry at St. James was quite different from the mission field in Russia. We saw the Lord do some great things, and lives were changed, but for the most part, we longed for the Lord to move here as He did in Russia.

An Encounter with God

The real-life event that you are about to read may sound wild - it was - but this actually happened to me, as surely as you are sitting there reading it! Buckle your seatbelt and get ready for take-off!

In our fourth year in Russia, we were pastoring our second church, in the city of Yaroslavl. We had a good team of American missionaries working with us, and we had morning prayer several days a week at our flat. For weeks we were experiencing something we had never seen before; it was that *Kabod* - "heavy" - presence of God! It was so thick that we all just lay on the floor.

Someone might ask, "Why lie on the floor?" My answer is, "We just couldn't stand up." This would last for hours. All of our former American teammates humorously refer to this as "Holy Ghost sunbathing."

It was during this time that I had an angelic visitation of a lifetime.

One morning after prayer, Rinalda and I (accompanied by our interpreter Anya) drove to the Yaroslavl train station. We pulled up to the train station and Rinalda, who was sitting shotgun, hopped out to go buy a chicken. Anya, who was seated in the back seat, got out to purchase tickets, and I waited in the car.

"The eyes of the Lord search the whole earth in order to strengthen those whose hearts are fully committed to Him..." 2 Chronicles 16:9 NLV

While I was looking to my left out the driver's side window at the half melted snow, I felt that familiar presence of God from our early morning prayer meetings. It quickly grew stronger and stronger, and as I turned my head to look straight ahead through the windshield, I saw the profile of two heads. They were so close, right between me and the steering wheel. They were the color of the sky on a clear day, that icy blue color. They had no hair, but I could make out both of their noses, eyes and ears. It was like I was caught up in another realm. I couldn't speak, but I felt unnaturally peaceful at the time. I felt totally focused on their presence.

As I turned slightly to the right, towards my stick shift, there was a third one; this one was facing directly at me and I could make out every feature of that icy-blue complexion.

All of a sudden I heard them say, "Don't be concerned; we will lead you, guide you, and show you what to do."

To this day, I can't tell you if they communicated to me in words or some other form of communication. There was no voice to remember, but I was sure of what they said. In an instant they were gone, as I heard the car door open and Rinalda got in, saying, "I got a chicken."

Anya hopped in the back seat and said, "Got the tickets."

I was in some type of shock, holding on to

consciousness, while at the same time trying to figure out where I was. I'm not sure if I could have spoken or tried to explain what happened. I was trying to figure out what country I was in, and trying to drive home.

Not a word was spoken all the way back to our flat. Upon arriving home, I went straight to my office, closed the door and tried to get a grip on reality.

Then my wife walked into the office and asked, "What happened in the car this morning?"

I said, "What do you mean? Why are you asking?"

She said, "When I opened the door, I literally felt the glory of God gush out of the car!" She said that it felt like she was standing on holy ground.

I was so thankful that she experienced that and helped validate this supernatural visitation of the Lord. Since that day, I knew deep down inside that the Holy Spirit's guidance throughout our lives was real, and I was just given that guarantee.

If you think that was wild, just read on.

It's Always Darkest Before the Dawn

It had been twenty years since my encounter with God in Russia. At this time we had been pastoring for eighteen years in America, and my real question was, "God, where are You? You met with me twenty years ago at a train station in Russia. You told me, 'Don't be concerned, we will lead you, guide you, and show you what to do.'"

I remember telling God, "I gave up everything. I followed You around the world. I've been serving You here for eighteen years, and two and a half years ago, You showed up in power, and now I can't find You anywhere. Have I done something wrong?"

It's quite humbling when you instantly realize that you are talking to God and you mentioned "I" five times in succession. Does anyone out there think that maybe "I" was the problem?

To make matters worse, I had been living in constant pain for the last seven years. Every morning when my feet hit the ground, I was in pain from the weight of my body. The doctors said I had degenerative cartilage. They unsuccessfully tried to burn the nerves in my back. They said that it was inoperable, and I was on 10 milligrams of hydrocodone four times a day, the maximum dose that could be prescribed.

With all that I was going through and all that I had previously experienced with God, I was now more desperate for Him than ever before.

Questions for Reflection:

1. **What situation in your life makes you ask the question, "God where are you?"**

2. **In that situation, is there any way that I can see God at work?**

Chapter 3

The Road to Dawsonville

Rinalda had been watching Sid Roth every night before bed, and she told me that there were three revivals across the South. Being a student of revival history, that quickly got my attention. I researched them all and said, "Honey, this one in Dawsonville, Georgia, is so 'out-of-the-box,' it has to be God!"

Pastor Todd Smith of Christ Fellowship Church had a vision of fire on the water of his baptismal; he said that God was meeting His people in the water! After pastoring for years, I had seen the effects of congregations putting God "in a box," and didn't want any part of that. The revival sounded so far from being in a box.

I want to remind you of the Bible's account of God parting the waters of the Red Sea to rescue His people (Exodus 14), causing water to gush out of a rock to give drink to His thirsty people (Exodus 20), and miraculously floating an ax head on water to help one of His people in distress (2 Kings 6). (Yes, there are so many more amazing "water stories" in the Bible.)

In the next couple of days, we were on the road

headed to Dawsonville! We arrived in time for their Sunday morning service, and they were having prayer in the main sanctuary before the service.

There was such anticipation that I knew something could happen, but just what would happen I had no idea. My mind raced with thoughts of how God had moved in power in our men's meetings, but that had been two and a half years ago.

Was God through with what He wanted to do with us, or would He bring real revival? There were so many questions and no answers. All I knew to do was to press forward.

The moment I entered the sanctuary, I sensed a strong presence of God. I was amazed to learn they had been having revival services every Sunday night for about a year, and five churches were involved with making it all come together. They took turns doing the preaching, music, and the children's ministry.

When I heard that, I knew this was God. My experience has been that two churches can't work together to change a roll of toilet paper without someone wanting the credit. However, people were walking around the main sanctuary praying silently with music in the background. There were revival quotes and scriptures on the overhead screen.

It was evident to me that prayer and unity were the keys to this movement of the Holy Spirit. I went to Dawsonville desperate for God and determined not to come home empty-handed. I went to a place in the sanctuary where I could be alone and pray.

A Prayer of Desperation

The great Welsh revival of 1902 was started by the prayer of young Evan Roberts when he prayed the famous prayer, "Lord, bend us; bend us, Lord." That morning, I prayed what I like to call "the Evan Roberts prayer on steroids." I prayed, "Lord, bend me, bend me, just break me; do whatever You need to; kill me if You have to; I have to have more of You, but Lord, if You kill me, would You take care of my wife and children?"

When I opened my eyes, I was still alive; it seemed that nothing had happened, but I was still desperate for His presence.

That night we returned for the Sunday night revival service. During the time of worship, I approached the platform and felt a hundred pounds heavier, so I lay down on the carpet. The next thing I knew, I was waking up and someone was preaching. I had been slain in the Spirit or "unconscious" for some time. I tried to get up, and two ushers helped me back to my seat.

When the baptism pool was open, both Rinalda and I waited in line to be baptized. As we stepped into the baptismal waters, we looked at each other and she said, "God is here in this water."

For a moment it was like, Is this really happening? When they were about to baptize me, I was asked,

"Who are you and what do you want God to do for you?"

I responded that I wanted the Holy Spirit to continue moving in our church the way He had been, and, at the last minute, I asked to be healed and off all my medication.

When I came out of the water, I was shaking uncontrollably all the way to the dressing room.

Healed and Free

The next morning when I woke up at the hotel, I got up, and as I began to walk around, I shouted, "Rinalda, get up; I'm healed!"

It seemed like a dream. God had healed me from seven years of constant pain! That day I drove ten hours back to Louisiana without taking any pain medication!

My first day back in Louisiana, I realized that God had given me back my life. For the next three days I was very tired, and I felt the need to take a nap. When I would raise my head I felt like I was lying on a cloud, like being in the hands of God!

A couple of weeks later I was telling my story to my friend who is a pharmacist, and he asked me about my withdrawals from the medicine. I told him, "Oh, I forgot I was supposed to go through withdrawals!"

I had heard stories from people I knew who had suffered through awful withdrawal symptoms after getting off prescribed meds like the ones I was on.

It was nothing nice, to say the least. Some have said that their skin felt like it was trying to crawl off their bones.

It's no secret today that there is a crisis in this country; Americans are hooked on drugs as a result of having been on strong pain meds. Through the mercy of my wonderful Savior, I was spared that!

How could I keep quiet? God had done for me what neurosurgeons and pain management physicians could not do! From the first day I was healed, I made it a priority to tell my story to anyone who wanted to listen. And that was on the average of five times per day!

Questions for Reflection:

1. **Does God still do miracles today?**

2. **Will God do a miracle in my life?**

3. **How desperate am I for my miracle?**

Chapter 4

You Can Eat Your Seed or Plant It

After returning home healed and having the excitement of revival in our hearts, all the events of Dawsonville seemed like a wonderful dream. I'd gotten my life back! Each day was filled with the excitement of a new opportunity to tell my story.

The first Sunday back in church, I stepped up to the pulpit and burst into tears. At the end of the message a number of people ran up for prayer. One man said, "Pray for me." I had no idea what he needed prayer for, but I touched him on the forehead with one finger and said, "Be healed in Jesus' name."

Instantly he burst into tears and went back to his seat. Later in the lobby, I asked him what happened when I prayed for him. He said that he was instantly healed, and he told me that he had so much arthritis in his body that he couldn't sleep at night. He said when I prayed for him, he felt something like electricity run through his whole body, and he was instantly healed!

Our weekly men's prayer and worship continued

with the "heavy" *Kabod* presence of God. At the end of one of our meetings one of our men asked for prayer; he'd been diagnosed with diabetes. Once again, it was a simple prayer. Two months later, his doctor confirmed that the diabetes was no longer there!

The Holy Spirit had already been moving in our church, but going to Dawsonville did more - it opened a door. When I was baptized, I asked God to move in our church again like He had before, and it was already happening.

The Bible says that God gives each of us a measure of faith (Romans 12:3); what we do with that faith is up to us. Faith is like a seed; you can plant your seed or not plant it. That measure of faith that God gives us was never meant to be hidden. We need to plant our faith, water it, watch it grow, and share it as much as possible.

When God answered my prayer, I had been given a new seed. Now I had the choice of eating my seed or planting it. Some of you already know where I'm headed with this. I could have come back with my healing and went on with my life, and things would be good. Instead I decided to plant what God had done for me in the lives of others.

Whatever God gives you, if you are willing to plant it, and ask God to water it, others can enjoy it, too. Being desperate for His presence, I decided to plant and harvest. The following is an account of how we planted the seed of revival fire.

The Birth of the Southeast Louisiana Revival

About two months after returning from Dawsonville, I just knew that I was supposed to hold a joint meeting with some other churches, but I had no idea what it would look like or how it would work. Most churches I knew didn't have joint meetings with other churches.

First, I laid out the vision with the men at our prayer group and then we prayed.

Next, I reached out to about ten pastors of nearby churches who knew about my healing and asked if they would join me to hold a three-day revival including water baptism. I told them that I believed God would do again what He was doing in Dawsonville. What I had seen in Dawsonville was that the Holy Spirit was honoring two things: prayer and unity.

I stepped out on the water.

I asked the pastors that I previously contacted to meet me for lunch to discuss the revival. Then I reached out to a pastor who I had had a very bad relationship with for the past fifteen years. In the past we tried to make things right, but it just never worked out until about four years ago when we reconciled.

The real question was, could we work together?

John 17:21 says, "*...that they would be as one.*" It was as plain as day what God wanted me to do, so I called this pastor and asked him to join our group.

I told him, "I really need you to make this happen, and without you it will not work."

He said, "OK, I'm in!"

That was the moment that I believe everything fell into place.

A total of five pastors attended our revival planning luncheon. This group became the hosts for the Southeast Louisiana Revival. I shared my whole story again, and we looked at the logistics and sizes of our various auditoriums.

The big questions were, How many people will possibly show up, and how will we baptize them all?

This was a moment of decision that would make it or break it. I decided to advertise it on FaceBook, and Pastor Todd, from Dawsonville, suggested putting up a fourteen-foot-wide Wal-Mart swimming pool in my auditorium. All the pastors just looked at me with no expression; It was a "frozen-in-time, Twilight Zone" moment!

Was there going to be a punch line?

I mean, how could you blame them? We were planning a joint revival meeting and putting up a fourteen-foot-wide Wal-Mart pool in the sanctuary!

We went on with the planning, and at the end of the meeting, all the pastors said they were one hundred percent on board.

But they did add that they were all glad that the

event was being held in my church.

Our first revival was set for the first weekend of May, 2019.

Pastor Todd Smith was our guest speaker and one of the cooperating pastors would lead worship with his worship team. The Wal-Mart pool was set up in our sanctuary and steps were built to enter and exit the pool.

Now, would God actually show up?

I remember going to buy the swimming pool and pulling it off the shelf. The moment I set it on the floor, I heard the enemy say, "I've got you now; I'll ruin you. You'll be a laughing stock. I can't wait for you to put this pool up!"

That's when courage rose up in me, and I knew I was going in the right direction! If the devil is that upset about what I'm doing, that means I'm going in the right direction. I have learned to discern his presence, too.

The First Night of Revival

The worship team arrived at our church two hours early to set up. People started arriving early, filling the building. Our building was full to capacity; there seemed to be people everywhere, and the air was filled with joyful anticipation. There was a real presence of God in the building!

I walked over to our Wal-Mart baptismal pool and as I touched the surface of the water, I burst into tears! That's when I knew for sure that this would be a historic night!

The evening began with the five Southeast Louisiana Revival pastors standing before the congregation in unity, thanking the Holy Spirit for His presence, and thanking everyone for coming.

The moment worship began, there was a real increase in the presence of God. Pastor Todd preached a powerful message and then Rinalda gave instructions on how the baptisms would be handled.

The Moment of Truth

With worship music in the background, people readied themselves for getting in the water, and formed a long line inside our building.

Our revival pastors were positioned around the outside of the pool, and people were eager to get in. I remember the first person on the top of the stairs getting ready to enter the water. At the moment her toe touched the water, she burst into tears.

In a couple of hours, there were scores of baptisms. Couples and whole families were being baptized together, as well as numerous individuals. I remember several times that as many as five people were being baptized simultaneously. At one point, one of our team members began waving his arms, shouting, "Too many people in the pool!"

We had to reorganize on the spot and limit the

number of people getting in. The presence of God was so powerful that some people were visibly dazed and stunned, unable to talk. Others put their faces in their hands and just sobbed. Some floated on their backs in the water, being supported in the arms of one of our ministers in the pool. Some told of how they were experiencing God's love in a powerful way.

People began getting in the water too quickly again, and we asked them to stand along the edge and wait to be baptized.

I asked some of our pastors who were baptizing to please get to the people waiting inside the pool next. By the time I turned around, a group of about six people waiting inside the pool were on their knees in the water.

They were gripping the edge of the pool and crying out to God for mercy. There were even reports of a swirling breeze of wind around the pool area! I couldn't believe my eyes. As a student of revival, I knew that these manifestations were indicative of those in the First and Second Great Awakenings.

The moment of truth had come, and God had shown Himself mighty, pouring Himself out on His people in various ways, meeting each person's individual needs.

Each night our building was filled to capacity, and we baptized until 1:00 in the morning! Many people who never got in the water at all were also touched by God.

There was an unusual sense of unity among the members of our church. We were hosting the event, we were doing all the work, we were serving everyone, but there was not one complaint. Everyone served over and above, working harder than we ever had - and it was a pleasure.

I was personally in a state of awe at what was taking place. Someone would come up and start talking and I would just say, "Look at what God is doing; isn't it just wonderful?"

Yes, it was and we were so excited that God had visited us in power!

The next three-day meeting was in July. This time we decided to invite Pastor Todd to come to different locations. God poured out his Spirit every bit as powerfully as before. He showed Himself mighty and held nothing back. Some of our prophetic ministry teams told us that they were able to flow freely in their prophetic giftings, just like the prophets did in the Bible.

Revival is Transferable

What we discovered is that revival is a fire that can be brought to a new location. Just as the torch was passed in the Olympics, we were about to pass revival fire all the way to Brazil.

Two of our Southeast Louisiana Revival pastors,

Donnie Shaffer and Mervin Strother, did just that. They said they were going to Brazil, and wanted to bring a pool to baptize there with fire and water.

In a couple of weeks their trip was put together; it turned out to be the mission trip of a lifetime! Armed with a portable pool from Wal-Mart, they traveled eight hours by plane and eleven hours by car with an overnight stop.

They called from Brazil and reported that in ten days they baptized 1,000 people and saw off-the-chart miracles!

Come on now, aren't those guys incredible! They just went for it and did it, and God showed up.

Flying Solo

In August, we began having revival meetings at St. James Community Church on the first Friday of the month. Each time we held a revival meeting, we asked a different pastor to preach and another church to lead worship. This was what I believe to be a real Holy Spirit-led decision.

Other churches were not only *feeling* like they were a part of what God was doing, they *actually were a* part of what God was doing. We all had this

wonderful thing in common: the experience of seeing God show up in His mighty power. We've been singing about it for years and now we have seen, up close, the manifestation of the Spirit of God responding to His people, and hearing, "I'm healed! I'm healed!"

Without a doubt I have seen more healings in this revival than I have in my whole Christian life.

But it's not just about the healings. In fact, the healings are just a side dish, so to speak, to the gourmet meal God is serving.

The big focus is God and how He is *really* meeting His people in the water. I believe with my whole being that everything we are seeing God do has come after years of prayer.

Questions for Reflection:

1. In what way has God already blessed me?

2. Have I used that blessing to bless others?

In Brazil: A Miracle for Aunt Isabel

For over 10 years, Aunt Isabel has had a serious back condition that worsened as time went on. She had been to the best doctors, including the orthopedic doctors. They said that the reason for her excruciating pain was that the cartilage in her vertebrae had worn away and was no longer there.

On her last doctor appointment she was told, "We can do no more for you; only God can heal you now." She heard about the revival and wanted to attend. The day before the revival baptisms, she had to receive injections in her back because she could no longer feel her feet.

Continued next page

Aunt Isabel – cont'd

At the revival, Pastors Donnie and Mervin were baptizing. One of them prayed for her, and as she came out of the water she passed out; she had to be carried out of the pool and placed on the ground.

When she turned red, the children said, "Aunt Isabel is either dead or she just got healed."

After she lay there for about twenty minutes covered with a red cloth, she jumped up and began to run and dance! The next day, she gave her testimony that she had been bedridden with headaches and backaches, and felt like she was always carrying a sack of cement. She said, "When I entered the water I asked Him to heal me, too. **I was healed immediately**."

PASTOR LARRY: After hearing her story, I feel like getting up and running around and dancing, myself!

Chapter 5

It All Began with Prayer

A year before my salvation, I was such a mess, and believe me I knew it.

I was 28 years old and no one had ever presented the gospel to me. That's right! Right here in America.

Raised as an Episcopalian, I later attended a Catholic boarding school, but I knew nothing about God. I know now that there were some people praying for me and, as a result of those prayers, I began having a strange desire to make a change in my life.

Somehow I thought that when people got their life straightened up, *then* they went to church. Boy, did I have it backwards?

So I started attending a local church in town. No matter what denomination or affiliation you mention, it's my experience that there are lifeless ones in them and ones with life. In hindsight, from my point of view, the church I was attending was dead, and I mean D E A D.

I had absolutely no idea that God was at work in that church, and I was about to have a personal encounter with the Holy Spirit! The people there were so happy to have a young person in their church that they had me working with the youth.

The LAST person that needed to be working with the youth was me; I was still drinking and doing drugs!

At the time, I had no problem with attending church. I got to church early on Sunday morning because I enjoyed having coffee with the men. I joined a Sunday school class and I had no clue what they were talking about.

In one of the young adult groups, I met a man who smiled at me all the time; in fact he smiled at me too much and it made me really uneasy. I knew I had to keep an eye on this character; I referred to him as "Mr. Smiley Face."

One day he approached me with that big grin and said, "We are so excited about you!"

All I could say was, "Okay." It was very uncomfortable to say the least.

Then he said, "We are praying for you."

I thanked him, but on the inside I was thinking, "The nerve of this guy; why does he think he needs to be praying for me?"

Please don't ever do that to anyone; it could come across as scary and do more harm than good. I'll get back to Mr. Smiley Face later.

One Saturday morning, I was home and I heard a

car pull up in my driveway. I looked out the window and I couldn't believe my eyes. It was "church people." I said, "Oh Lord, help me! The church people are at my door."

I didn't know they regularly visited new members, and besides, I'd been drinking and partying the night before, so I politely did my best to put them off, and got rid of them.

This church had what they called an early morning men's prayer breakfast. Sometimes it was held at the church. Other times, someone would host it at their home. It was great: only one opening prayer, lots of food, and just sitting around talking. I even hosted a couple of breakfasts at my home.

Then one day, I attended one at the church. There may have been twenty-five men there, and, as I walked in, one of the older men was blowing a duck call and everyone was laughing and talking.

I found a place to sit and settled in just in time for the opening prayer. The men on either side of me extended their hands so that we could join hands in prayer. Just as I grabbed their hands, I felt from both sides a jolt of power hit me so hard that I let their hands go and screamed, "Did you feel that?"

Every eye at the table looked at me in total shock. I looked at everyone to either side of me and said, "Never mind."

As we continued breakfast I would catch someone looking my way from time to time. When breakfast ended, an older gentleman approached and said, "It was God."

I asked, "What? What was God?" He looked me straight in the eye and said, "Son, it was God that touched you today."

Come on, somebody! I mean, was God after me or what? That rattled me so bad that I decided I was not coming back to church.

About this same time, Mr. Smiley Face had been asking me to come to a prayer meeting at his home. He said that there were a few people getting together for prayer and Bible study.

A Simple Prayer Healed Glaucoma

Toby has been a member of St. James Community Church for nineteen years.

From the beginning, God has been touching his life with blessing after blessing. They say that you can have everything, but if you don't have your health, you have nothing.

One day, Toby was diagnosed with glaucoma by two doctors.

- continued, next page -

I went, but honestly, it was only because he kept after me. The Bible study went well. I thought it wasn't so bad after all, and then they said, "Let's all join hands, close our eyes, and pray."

We gathered in a circle and several people prayed. Then Mr. Smiley Face said,

"Oh Jesus, we know that you are right here this very moment in our midst."

Well I peeked, and I didn't see anyone but us praying.

That was about enough to push me over the edge for good! I thought, "These people think Jesus is really there." I had no idea that He *really* was standing there.

After that I ran hard from God for another year. Then one day, in desperation, I attended a different church that I heard was moving in

A Simple Prayer Continued

At this time we were in our sixth month of the revival. Toby came to our weekly men's prayer group and told us his situation. We told him, "Let's not speak the word glaucoma right now; let us pray and see what God does."

He was already scheduled to see a specialist to decide how they would treat the glaucoma, but that night, four men gathered around Toby and prayed a simple prayer.

When Toby went to the specialist, there was no longer any evidence of glaucoma!

Why don't you just give the Lord a shout right now, wherever you are! What a GREAT GOD WE SERVE!!!

the power of the Holy Spirit.

To my surprise, guess who met me in the foyer of the new church.

None other than Mr. Smiley Face himself.

I thought, "This guy is relentless!"

But it was there in the company of people like him who, yes, relentlessly pursue God, that the walls came down - that I surrendered my life to the Lord Jesus Christ - and received salvation.

I understood then that it was what I was looking for all my life, a relationship with the one true God.

When I think about this story now, I know that there were people praying for me, and those prayers led to my initial encounter with the presence of the living God.

So, back to my comment that God was what I was really looking for all my life.

On that note, I have a story that I think you would be encouraged to hear.

Fast forward to 1992. My wife and I were on the mission field in the Russian city of Furmanov, planting our first church.

Throughout my initial trips to that city, I met a rock and roll band and prayed with most of the members for salvation.

Can you guess what comes next? Yes, this band would later become our worship team!

On one of my trips there, I was tired and ready to go home, but the leader of their band insisted that I needed to meet their drummer and pray for him.

When we arrived there, it was my first time to enter an old Russian home of that type. The drummer's mother escorted us down a dingy hall into a small room where a man was drumming on a coffee table.

After introductions, we spoke just a few minutes about a real God that cared about him and wanted to have a relationship with him. He readily accepted Jesus as the Lord of his life.

What he told me is something I'll never forget.

He said, "I've been looking for this all my life."

His name is Slava and it means "glory." At that time Slava was about to be divorced. He and his wife Olga had a baby daughter named Masha.

Well, we all know that Jesus changes lives. Slava went on to Bible college, and he and Olga are not only happily married now, but they pastor a church in Russia. Their daughter Masha is a fabulous worship leader.

People don't realize it, but what they are *really* looking for is the living God. Only He can fill that void in their lives. We are called to pray for the lost, and God will open the door for their salvation.

Now I know that Mr. Smiley Face had people praying for me.

Thank God!

As for Slava, he had a rock and roll band praying for him. Prayer works, because at the other end of each prayer is a God who hears them and loves to answer them.

Questions for Reflection:

1. Is my prayer life where it needs to be?

2. What is the greatest obstacle to my prayer life?

Chapter 6

The Greatest Secret Weapon

The greatest secret weapon of every believer is the power of prayer. The problem is that, for the most part, God's people rarely use this great weapon unless it's their last resort.

We have all, at one time or another, found ourselves in a desperate situation, and heard someone say, "Well, all we can do now is pray!"

That scenario sums up our true feelings about the importance of prayer.

As Christians, we all say that we believe in the importance of prayer; however, our actions prove otherwise.

Let's face it, if the church announces a potluck dinner, every member will be in attendance with their extended family and a few possible new church members. But, if we hold a prayer meeting, everyone has a previously scheduled event.

On one hand, we know the great promises of God about prayer, but on the other hand we neglect using this great power that God has given us.

If I have gotten your attention let's take a look at both sides of the issue.

In America, one out of every six people takes antidepressants, but God's Word says, "Don't be anxious, pray about it!"

> Philippians 4:6-7, "*Be anxious for nothing, but in everything by prayer and supplication, with thanksgiving, let your requests be made known to God; and the peace of God, which surpasses all understanding, will guard your hearts and minds through Christ Jesus*" (NKJV).

All of us have concerns about our country and the area in which we live, but God's Word says to pray and seek Him!

> 2 Chronicles 7:14, "*If My people who are called by My name will humble themselves, and pray and seek My face, and turn from their wicked ways, then I will hear from Heaven, and will forgive their sin and heal their land*" (NKJV).

It's really not hard to get to Heaven, but it sure is hard living here on earth.

We all tend to try facing life alone, when God desires for us to ask Him for our needs. His Word says that we should ask Him:

> James 4:2 "...*you do not have because you do not ask*" (NKJV)

God doesn't respond to whining, moaning or complaining; He responds to faith. Faith is simply having the confidence that your heavenly Father that loves you will provide for you. You may not know how He will do it, but you know that He will. God's Word says that we have this confidence!

> 1 John 5:14 *"Now this is the confidence that we have in Him, that if we ask anything according to His will, He hears us. 15 And if we know that He hears us, whatever we ask, we know that we have the petitions that we have asked of Him"* (NKJV)

One of the greatest keys to answered prayer is faith. Mark 11:24 gives us great insight into just how faith works. God's Word says that the thing that we are praying for, we need to believe that it's already been provided. It has already been decreed in Heaven; the miracle is already done in the heavenly realm. You are just waiting for the delivery!

The greatest secret weapon of every believer is the power of prayer.

Look closely at Mark 11:24, read it, re-read it, and meditate on it until it becomes revelation:

> Mark 11:24, *"Therefore I say to you, whatever things you ask when you pray, believe that you receive them, and you*

will have them" (NKJV).

Answering the Big Question

These are only a few of the scriptures concerning God's promises about prayer.

God says that He will answer prayer; the problem is He doesn't say when. Some people believe that you pray the prayer of faith one time, and if you keep asking, that is a lack of faith. If that is true, what do we do with the parable of the persistent widow?

The story is about a widow who persistently goes before an unjust judge, asking for help. Let's look at the story:

Luke 18:1-8 *"Then He spoke a parable to them, that men always ought to pray and not lose heart, saying: "There was in a certain city a judge who did not fear God nor regard man. Now there was a widow in that city; and she came to him, saying, 'Get justice for me from my adversary.' And he would not for a while; but afterward he said within himself, 'Though I do not fear God nor regard man, yet because this widow troubles me I will avenge her, lest by her continual coming she weary me.' Then the Lord said, "Hear what the unjust judge said. And shall God not avenge His own elect who cry out day and night to Him, though He bears long with them? I tell you that He will avenge them speedily. Nevertheless, when the Son of Man comes, will He really find faith on the earth?"* (NKJV)

This story paints a picture of what real faith is.

Real faith is knowing that, sooner or later, God will answer. He will vindicate you; He will come to your rescue. Real faith is being persistent until the miracle arrives!

How is it that we know that we have to be persistent to obtain a degree, or to build a business, or to have a great marriage, but in the area of prayer we want an instant answer or we call it quits?

A Miracle for Spike

Spike suffered from the pain of a damaged rotator cuff and was scheduled for surgery. On visiting one of our Southeast Louisiana Revival services, Spike knew that he was going to meet God in the water! When he was baptized, he knew God had touched him. A few days later, he went to the doctor and said, "Doc, you believe in miracles?" He then raised both arms straight up in the air and the doctor said, "Yes, I believe in miracles."

After an MRI, the doctor said that it looked 90 percent healed and asked if Spike wanted him to go in and clean it up a bit. Spike said, "No let's just leave it like it is."

Today, Spike is one hundred percent healed!

The average believer is familiar with all these scriptures; however, the vast majority of believers have very little to no personal prayer life at all.

How is it that most believers almost never attend a prayer meeting?

The answer is really simple: prayer is just not natural! Think about it; if you are having a conversation with someone that you can't see, feel or touch, you do all the talking and no one answers back!

That's just not natural. That's because, **in the case of prayer, it's SUPERNATURAL**!

Prayer is a supernatural event! When we pray, we are having supernatural conversation with the Creator of the universe, our heavenly Father who loves us.

> **"God shapes the world by prayer. The more praying there is in the world, the better the world will be, and the mightier the forces against evil."** — *E.M. Bounds*

At the writing of this book, my wife and I have pastored this church for nineteen years. God began to pour out His Spirit here about three years ago, but it was one year ago that revival began. I believe that it was a result of a combination of things: seven years of men's prayer, early morning prayer and worship, and the prayers of couples in our church who have prayed for this area for the past thirty years.

When you keep on going and you refuse to give

up, sooner or later you arrive at the destination. The key is not giving up!

When God first showed up, it was in the presence of His Holy Spirit, then came the revival!

We have learned that prayer is our powerhouse and quitting is never an option.

No matter who you are - if you are a pastor, a minister, a husband, a wife - if He's given you a business, a job, a position, quitting is not an option!

When we hit hard times, we need to stop and ask ourselves, did God give us this position, this marriage, this ministry? If you can think back to the time that you were excited because you knew God put you there, it's certainly not time to quit!

You are just going through a season, but seasons end and you get through to the other side if you just press in and don't give up!

Questions for Reflection:

1. What is the one area of your life that could only change through a divine miracle of God?

2. Are you willing to press in daily in prayer until you receive your miracle?

Chapter 7

Great Moves of God Were All Birthed by Prayer

It's difficult to think of American Christianity apart from revivals. Historians actually divide American church history by the different times of revivals that they refer to as the "Great Awakenings."

"To desire revival... and at the same time to neglect (personal) prayer and devotion is to wish one way and walk another."
— A.W. Tozer

The word "revival" is defined in Webster's Dictionary as a period of renewed religious interest: an often highly emotional evangelistic meeting or series of meetings.

The First Great Awakening 1720-1760s

Jonathan Edwards was the brilliant and wildly popular pastor of the North Hampton Church in

Massachusetts. His method of preaching lacked enthusiasm, but when he fixed his eyes on the back wall of the sanctuary, the Holy Spirit moved. His words became so powerful that they sank deep into the hearts of the congregation.

His preaching is generally credited with paving the way for the first great awakening!

"Prayer is as natural an expression of faith as breathing and necessary for revival."
- Jonathan Edwards

In Herrnhut, Germany, in 1727, the Moravians, along with about 300 refugees, began unified prayer that brought about a great hunger for Jesus and His Word. They desired, above all else, that the Holy Spirit would have full control of their lives. They experienced the forsaking of self-love, self-will, and disobedience.

Then it was as if an overwhelming flood of grace swept them into a great ocean of divine love. This resulted in an all night prayer watch that continued one hundred years and birthed the first systematic dispatch of missionaries around the world.

The Moravians knew that prayer was their powerhouse and that quitting was never an option.

The most notable figure of that first great

awakening was George Whitefield, from England. He is considered one of the fathers of the Methodist church. He was known as the silver-tongued preacher of the American colonies, and wherever he preached, revival started.

Newspapers dubbed him, "the marvel of the age." Whitefield's sermons did not focus on the religious doctrines of the day. Instead, he focused on the hearts of the people.

The established church quickly closed their doors to him and he was forced to hold open-air meetings. When Whitefield came to town, everything shut down and the whole population assembled in the town square. He once preached to 23,000 people, and, we have to remember, there were no microphones. It was a supernatural event.

In one year, he traveled 5,000 miles and preached 350 sermons. He also did seven tours through the colonies, preaching 18,000 sermons.

It is estimated that in his lifetime ten million people heard him preach! George Whitefield knew that prayer was his powerhouse and quitting was never an option.

In 1735, the meetings of Jonathan Edwards had a deep effect on the hearts and minds of New Englanders. Day after day, lost souls flocked to Jesus in great numbers finding the joy of their salvation and a deep concern for the souls of their neighbors.

Jonathan Edwards' most famous message was, "Sinners in the Hands of an Angry God." According to eyewitness accounts, Edwards' sermon was so effective that it was interrupted by loud shrieks and wails of people in the congregation. His listeners actually felt that the church pews lifted up, causing an overwhelming sense of falling into the pits of Hell.

The most important piece of doctrine in Edwards' message - the hope of salvation from Hell by dedication to God - was barely heard over the noise of the crowd. Edwards, too, knew that prayer was his powerhouse, and quitting was never an option.

Now let's jump across the pond and see what was happening in Jolly Old England in that era.

In the late 1720s, John Wesley and his brother Charles attended Oxford University. It was during that time that they started a group known, in mockery, to fellow colleagues as the "Holy Club."

On Wednesdays and Fridays, they fasted until 3:00 pm. Each week, they received communion together and discussed the Greek New Testament. They also participated in a personal accountability group, visited the sick and those who were in prison.

This group never exceeded twenty-five members. One of the members of this group was none other than George Whitefield. The Methodist church can trace its roots back to that original group. Each week, John Wesley's group would meet for fellowship, prayer and study; they also met for the purpose of personal accountability. In their group, each person would be asked the following questions as it pertained to their personal life:

1. **What known sins have you committed since our last meeting?**

2. **What temptations have you met with?**

3. **How were you delivered?**

4. **What have you thought, said, or done, of which you doubt whether it be sin or not?**

In 1739, John Wesley and George Whitefield held meetings where entire crowds fell to the ground as if they were struck by thunder. Their meetings were marked with enthusiastic singing, powerful preaching, crowds gripped with conviction, repentance and weeping. The numbers of attendees swelled to 50,000 at open meetings on hillsides, with untold thousands being saved.

As you can see, these men were serious about their walk with the Lord, leaving no advantage for the enemy in their personal lives. This is how they were able to accomplish extraordinary things for the Lord.

John and Charles Wesley took tunes commonly sung in their day and added godly lyrics to them. This is commonly known today as a piggyback song. Many of the Wesleys' piggyback songs became the great hymns that we know today.

John Wesley was not allowed in Anglican pulpits, so he preached in open air meetings to tens of thousands. Though small in stature – five-foot six and 120 pounds - he crisscrossed England on horseback, covering 250,000 miles preaching the Gospel.

John Wesley also knew that prayer was his powerhouse and that quitting was never an option.

In 1781, in Cornwall, England, concerts of prayer were held each evening until midnight, impacting the nation with social change and creating a climate for political reform. It was prayer that moved the Holy Spirit, which prompted William Wilberforce to be used by God to abolish slavery in the United Kingdom. "Amazing Grace" writer, John Newton became a supporter of and inspiration to William Wilberforce.

As in other instances, the people of Cornwall learned that prayer was their powerhouse, and quitting was never an option.

The Second Great Awakening 1790-1840

Charles Finney started out as an attorney with no theological training. Even though he led the choir in a small church, he was not saved, and the young people were warned not to be influenced by his ungodly ways. I would say that there were people praying for young Mr. Finney, because it wasn't long before he fell under a deep conviction over his own personal sin.

In his autobiography, The *Autobiography of Charles G. Finney: The Life Story of America's Greatest Evangelist--In His Own Words*, Finney talked about going out to a secluded place in the woods to "see about the condition of my soul."

In other words, he went there to repent and get right with God! When he returned to his small office, he said that he met Jesus face to face. He described his encounter this way: "As a man looks at another man."

Falling to his knees he was overcome with what he described as "waves of love that would not cease."

In the area of upstate New York, where Finney preached, the Calvinists taught that you could only receive salvation if God had elected you to be saved. Once again, the doors of the traditional church were closed to what the Holy Spirit was doing.

Finney was responsible for what the Calvinists called "New Measures." He believed that anyone could hear a gospel message, repent of their sins, accept Christ as Lord and receive the assurance of your salvation.

Hey, that sounds good to me!

The traditional church was further outraged because he allowed women to pray in public. He held church meetings on weekdays, which was scandalous in the day! He instituted the first altar call where people came forth to receive salvation.

Altar calls were later used by the great revivalists Billy Sunday and D. L. Moody.

Finney also allowed new believers to become members of the church. With this long list of Finney's irreverent approach to the gospel, there was one other thing that made their religious heads fall off and roll on the floor. Mr. Finney instituted the "anxious bench." This was a certain bench that people would sit on when they felt that the Holy Spirit was moving upon them to get right with God. From that bench people would next receive Christ as Savior.

I think we might need a few of these benches in our churches today!

The upper region of New York state was transformed under Finney's ministry. He was called the greatest American evangelist. His revival ministry spanned fifty years, with over a half-million people converted under his preaching.

He preached repentance and holiness, and the spirit of conviction would fill the audiences with moaning and groaning.

When he came to town, entire populations came to Christ as Savior and barrooms were literally shut down.

What was the power behind his ministry? It was the power of prayer that preceded Finney in each town.

A man named Nash would travel to each town prior to Finney's arrival and would spend long hours in prayer for the town's salvation. Mr.Nash would find a secluded place and kneel down in the snow, throwing his cloak over his back. After he finished lengthy prayer time and arose from his kneeling position, there would be an imprint of his body and cloak and a stain of blood in the snow, where he had coughed up blood from his tuberculosis.

Charles Finney knew that prayer was his powerhouse, and quitting was never an option.

At the latter part of the Second Great Awakening, in 1801, revival came to a town called Cane Ridge, near Lexington, Kentucky. People were drawn to a place in the woods near Cane Ridge until 12,500 people were assembled there. Eyewitnesses reported that there were seven ministers preaching at the same time in various locations, some standing on a stump or a buckboard. They reported that there was a noise like the roar of Niagara Falls.

At one time, over 500 people were swept down, in a moment, as if a battery of a thousand guns had opened up upon them. People were falling down, crying out, trembling, groaning and crying for mercy. This final push of the Second Great Awakening produced the modern missionary movement and its societies that added untold thousands into His Kingdom.

The people of Cane Ridge knew that prayer was

their powerhouse, and quitting was never an option.

The Third Great Awakening 1857-1930

The first two great awakenings began in the pulpits of America, but the third great awakening began in a businessman's prayer meeting. This is how it all started.

There was a small church in South Carolina, comprised of forty-eight former slaves pastored by John Girardeau. One night the Spirit of God fell in that place and the prayer meeting grew to about 2000 people.

In that meeting was a young man whose name was Jeremy Lanphier. Jeremy moved to New York where, as a businessman, he made 2,000 invitations at his own expense and invited businessmen to a noontime prayer meeting. At his first meeting there were only six men in attendance.

God's Word says, **"*Do not despise these small beginnings, for the Lord rejoices to see the work begin*"** (Zechariah 4:10 NLT)

In his next meeting there were twenty men in attendance. Each meeting, the numbers doubled and tripled, so that the number of meeting places grew. They grew so much that soon they were all over New York City!

The structure of the meeting was simple: there was

a five minute rule, anyone could stand and pray but the prayer could not exceed five minutes. One reporter traveled between locations by horse and buggy to count how many people were attending the different prayer locations. He counted 6,000 before the noontime meeting was over.

On one particular day, it was reported that someone passed a written prayer request through the group for others to read. One lady had written, "I'm a Christian, and please, please pray for my unsaved husband."

After a moment of silence one man jumped to his feet and said, "I'm that man!"

Then another man jumped to his feet and said, "No No, I'm sure that I'm that man!"

Other men rose to their feet and said, "No, I know that I'm that man!"

In that one meeting alone, 600 men were saved!

A noontime prayer meeting that began with one businessman soon became 6,000 men praying!

Even the ships that entered the harbor experienced the presence of God. What happened aboard these ships came from one sea captain on a sinking ship; he lashed himself to some boards and promised, "God, if you save me, I'll serve you."

It is reported that during the 1858-1859 revival, a million souls were saved.

This businessman's noontime prayer meeting

became known as the Fulton Street revival, and somehow reached around the world.

In 1850, in Ulster, Ireland, a young schoolboy named James McQuilkin came under strong conviction and announced to his classmates, "Oh, I'm so happy because I have the Lord Jesus in my heart." Subsequently, bitter weeping spread throughout the whole school, and soon the whole school was saved.

This same soul-saving revival spread around the globe, and in 1859 in Natal, South Africa, revival began to spread among the Zulu tribes. An African servant girl sang and prayed in a meeting and the Holy Spirit fell on the whole group. It was reported that a roaring sound like approaching thunder surrounded the hall where they met and began to shake it.

This certainly sounds familiar; it sounds like the Cane Ridge revival. It even sounds like what we personally experienced at St. James Community Church in Paulina, Louisiana.

"Do not despise these small beginnings, for the Lord rejoices to see the work begin." Zechariah 4:10 NLT

Interestingly, the day that Jeremy Lanphier started his first noontime prayer meeting was September 23, 1857. On that very same day **in eight**

countries around the world, it was recorded that something significant happened concerning prayer

and revival. Jeremy Lanphier knew that prayer was his powerhouse, and to him, quitting was never an option.

I personally believe that the Fulton Street businessman's prayer meeting in New York was the birthplace for the revival decade of 1900-1910.

The wind of the Holy Spirit carried the revival fire from nation to nation. The wonderful news of the Welch revival reached prayer groups around the world. Wales, England, Scotland, Scandinavia, Europe, South Africa, India, Korea, South America, China, Indonesia, Japan, Australia, New Zealand, and North America were all touched, with countless millions being saved.

We cannot talk about the subject of prayer and revival without mentioning Evan Roberts and the Welch revival.

Young Evan Roberts was a coal miner that God used to turn all of Wales back to Himself. Early each morning for a three-month period, from 1:00 to 5:00 am, Evan was awakened by the Lord. He said that during these early morning hours he met with the Lord face to face, "as a man meets with his friend."

In a church service one day, the Lord told him that 100,000 souls would be saved. Evan prayed the famous prayer, "Lord, bend us; bend us, Lord!"

This revival was not characterized by dynamic preaching like early revivals. This was a revival of

prayer, singing, many salvations and intense presence of the Lord. It was said that when one crossed the border from England and stood on Welch territory, he could actually feel the presence of the Lord. The country was so affected that the police department was disbanded due to a lack of crime.

Someone asked a group of policemen at the revival if they were there for crowd control. "No," they answered, "we have a policeman's choir. We are singing in the revival!"

When the miners got saved, they stopped cursing and beating the mules that pulled the coal wagons. The change was so drastic that the miners had to purchase new mules that would respond to the miners who no longer cursed their commands.

Elections were cancelled because everyone was at the revivals. The country's soccer championship was not held during the years of revival because everyone was, guess where? They were at the revival!

Evan Roberts knew that prayer was his powerhouse, and quitting was never an option.

The Azusa Street Revival

The Azusa Street revival was led by William Seymore, an African American holiness preacher who lost one eye to smallpox as a child. He had very little education, but he loved the Lord and was determined to serve Him.

Seymore spent long hours in prayer and he was known for using two apple crates that were nailed together for his pulpit. He would rest his head inside the crate for a time before he began to preach.

His church was a 40' x 60' building that had been used as a horse stable. His pews were planks of wood nailed to a barrel on each end.

We all know what a horse stable smells like, but God was there.

From these humble beginnings came the most well known revival of the 20th century. It took place in 1906 at 312 Azusa Street in Los Angeles, California, and the revival continued until 1915. The Azusa Street revival gave birth to the Charismatic Pentecostal movement and launched it around the world.

People from all points of the globe and from every walk of life came to the Azusa Street revival. Six hundred million people and twelve denominations trace their spiritual roots to this revival.

The eyewitness accounts of what took place at this revival are nothing short of miraculous! There were reports of people from other countries hearing, in their own languages, people speaking in tongues about the Glory of God.

There were numerous accounts of the deaf hearing

and the blind receiving their sight. One lady whose eyes were not developed from birth received her healing and saw for the first time. One man who lost his arm at the shoulder in a factory accident, was prayed for, and his arm grew back, first with bones, and then with flesh that covered the arm and his hand. This was witnessed by a group of believers.

On numerous occasions, passersby saw fire on the roof of the Azusa Street church and called for the fire department, only to learn that the blaze was the fire of the Holy Spirit. There were nights when a cloud of glory rested inside the building, and eyewitnesses, in later years, said that as children they played hide and seek in the glory cloud.

William Seymore knew that prayer was his powerhouse, and quitting was never an option.

The Hebrides Revival

Jumping forward in time almost fifty years, let's look at one of my most favorite revivals.

From 1949 to1953, in the Hebrides Islands off the coast of Scotland, two aged sisters prayed night and day, fanning the flames of revival. These two sisters were eighty- two and eighty-four years old.

Hey, don't ever think that you are too old to do something significant!

The prayers of Christine and Peggy Smith that were offered up day and night began a chain reaction. Their prayers caused six or seven men in a barn to pray three nights a week from 10:00 pm to 3:00 am.

One of the sisters had a vision of many young people in the church she attended and the sanctuary being filled to capacity all the way to the back of the church, and she envisioned a strange man standing in the pulpit. The sisters had gotten a clear word from the Lord that said, "*I will pour water on him that is thirsty, and floods upon the dry ground*" (Isaiah 44:3).

One night in the barn where the men had been praying, one of the young deacons from the church stood and read Psalm 24:3-5 "*Who may climb the mountain of the Lord? Who may stand in his holy place? Only those whose hands and hearts are pure, they will receive the Lord's blessing...*" (Not "A" blessing, but "THE" blessing of the Lord.)

At that moment, the deacon stood and said, "Here we are praying and praying, waiting and waiting, but God is saying, 'Are we right with Him?'"

Suddenly, they all knew that the revival was about holiness. The young deacon fell to his knees, and went quickly into a trance. The power of God swept into the parish and an awareness of God gripped the community such as had not been known in one hundred years.

The next day, very little work was done on any farm, looms were silent and men and women gave themselves to concerns about eternal things, being gripped by eternal realities.

It was an invitation that brought Duncan Campbell to Lewis Island in the Hebrides. The night of his arrival, he was asked to speak at a church with 300 people in attendance. The meeting went from 9:00 pm to about 11:00 pm. When he closed the meeting and walked outside, he was astonished to find 600 people standing outside, having been unable to get inside.

It was prayer that primed the pump and began a Holy Spirit outpouring, drawing people from all over the parish. There were about one hundred young people that were attending a dance. Those attending the dance said that the music stopped and the Spirit of God fell in the dance hall, sending people running out of the hall and toward the church.

Just as the old lady had seen in the vision, the church did get filled with young people; however she had no idea that they would be lying prostrate on the floor crying for mercy.

There were many eyewitness accounts of 400 people showing up that very night at the police station, confessing their sins and asking God for mercy.

The Smith sisters learned that prayer was their powerhouse, and quitting was never an option.

One of the most fascinating stories that have come out of the Hebrides revival is the story of Donald Trump's mother, who was born and raised there and immigrated to New York. It turns out that

Donald Trump's mother, whose maiden name was Mary Anne Smith MacLeod, was the niece of Christine and Peggy Smith - the famous intercessors of the Hebrides Revival.

These Islands were so affected by God that all the inhabitants were saturated in God's presence for years to come. It is reported that a Bible President Trump has in the Oval Office today is the same Bible sent to his mother from the Hebrides Islands Revival many years ago.

In this chapter, I gave you the highlights of only a few of the great revivals throughout history. The purpose of this chapter was to bring out some life-changing points to remember:

1. **Revivals change the course of history.**

2. **Prayer spawns revivals.**

3. **Lack of prayer causes revivals to end.**

4. **Revivals are not all the same.**

Let's examine these truths one at a time.

Revivals change the course of history.

It is well documented that in the days of Jonathan Edwards, the colonists had reached a place of moral depravity. Revival brought about a "deep sense of God awareness" that remained for years to come.

Think about the people of Cornwall, England, and

William Wilberforce. It was a revival of prayer that brought an end to slavery in the United Kingdom.

It was revival among the Moravians that caused one

hundred years of prayer that kicked off the first missionary societies. It was the Fulton Street Businessman's prayer revival that launched revivals around the world, and when men's hearts are changed, it always affects society in a good way!

Prayer spawns revivals.
Jonathan Edwards' ministry was affected

A Miracle for Pastor Bryan Keelin

Pastor Bryan, of Vineyard Church in Carencro, Louisiana, attended our first revival meeting on May 1, 2019. He had been suffering with a damaged rotator cuff since December of 2018, and was in tremendous pain. Without insurance he was reluctant to incur the cost of seeing a doctor.

When he entered the baptism waters at our church, he felt the presence of God in the water!

- continued -

---

by a prayer movement in Scotland that mobilized the American church to commit to seven years of prayer. John Wesley recorded in his journal that he and his friends prayed through the night and that some were filled with joy while others were thrown to the ground.

There was one exceptional night of prayer that so

affected Wesley that, around 3:00 am, he was said to be propelled out of the room like a meteor!

William Seymore would have been nominated the least likely to succeed in ministry. When he attended Charles Parham's Bible School, he was not allowed to sit in the classroom because he was black. He was, however, allowed to sit outside the door and listen to the lectures. In the eyes of some, his race disqualified him, but being a man that prayed three hours per day qualified him to lead the greatest revival of the twentieth century.

Lack of prayer ends revivals. It is the nature of man that, when God blesses us, we get our attention on the blessing and forget the One from whom the blessing came. If we focus on seeking His face and not what is in His hand, we can continue in His presence.

Revivals are not all the same. A revival is an

answer to prayer; it is God lovingly blessing us with His presence. It is as if God leans down from

Heaven and gives us a kiss. God's Word says that it's foolish to compare ourselves to others. When we look at revivals throughout history we discover that each revival is unique in its own way.

They do have certain similarities, but they all have their differences. Sometimes I'll hear someone say, "If it were a real revival, they would meet every night."

That usually comes from someone who is recalling one experience in his life and is trying to apply it to what God is doing in different places and in different times.

One interesting pattern that we see throughout history is that, when one generation experiences a new move of God, many of those people become the persecutors of the next move of God.

Some believe that if God is going to do something, He will surely do it the way "I" have seen Him do it before.

From what I have seen, God can do anything He wants, He can use anyone He wants to use, and He is always full of surprises. We serve an exciting and wonderful God!

In our experience, the best night for us to have our revivals is on the first Friday night of every month. This gives our prayer team the time to meet each week to pray for the revival. Our cooperating churches have time to coordinate the worship teams so that have a continuing flow of the Holy Spirit.

Questions for Reflection:

1. **What type of people did God use to birth revivals?**

2. **Could God use me to spark a revival?**

Chapter 8

One-Eyed Snakes, the Missing Link, and Little Clubs

We have all heard of the great plagues of London in 1665. These plagues had been occurring for centuries. People of the day had many theories of what caused them. Some believed they were a punishment from an angry God. Some of the religious reformist groups of the day, such as the Puritans, blamed the Church of England for being too extravagant. The Catholic population of England blamed the plague on its congregants who strayed from strict religious ways.

Others believed that bad odors were the source of the disease. So they encouraged people to burn incense or hold sweet smelling flowers to their faces to prevent the disease. Physicians used medical techniques, such as bloodletting, boil-lancing, and superstitious practices like burning aromatic herbs or bathing in rose water and vinegar.

There were also some upper-class men who joined processions of flagellants traveling from town to town engaging in public displays of penance. In an attempt to win favor with God, they would beat themselves with leather straps while the townspeople looked on. This ritual was performed three times per day. After a time they would move on to the next town.

Back then no one could have ever guessed that the true source of the plague was a flea riding on a rat infected with the bacteria. When the host rat died, the flea would leave the rat and bite a person, transferring the bacteria. Now just hold that thought!

In our day all churches are doing their best – or *should* be - to fulfill the Great Commission. Jesus has left us with the task of reaching our world with the gospel of Jesus Christ. I mean come on, Jesus can't return until we finish the task.

Our churches are trying everything we can try, and doing all that we can do. Whichever church seems to be growing the most, we want to use their formula so that we can have the results they are having. Church leaders will travel across the globe to learn how to implement the new leadership material that promises the fastest growth.

Christian magazines have articles like "Five Barriers to Church Growth," or "Three Easy Steps to Grow Your Congregation."

Almost every pastor that I know feels like they take one step forward and three steps back. So why is it so hard to reach people with the gospel today?

Why is there not a stronger move of the Spirit? Why do we see so few miracles? Why do we see so few people really respond to the Lord in real commitment? Could there possibly be an answer to this problem that we would never suspect?

The One-Eyed Snake

As in the case of the Londoners of their day, could the answer be something that we would never guess?

We could blame it on people's obsession with sports, little league, FaceBook, materialism, and the list goes on. Have we become like the people of London who had no idea that the answer to the plague was right under their noses? Maybe we need to look beyond what we think we understand.

Consider this: could the Body of Christ be blind to a simple but profound common denominator, such as the lack of unity among believers?

Could that be why Christianity is not changing the world like it has the awesome, unbridled power to do?

What?

No way! That's ludicrous!

Really. Let's entertain this thought for a moment.

The Bible says that God is love, and without forgiveness you cannot even receive salvation. As ministers, we tell people all the time that your life will never be what it could be if you don't walk in forgiveness. It's the essence of Christianity.

Unforgiveness Bridles

With all that in mind, think about it; there are pastors who won't talk to each other, members of the same church who won't speak to each other, and church organizations that label other church organizations heretics over which version of the Bible they use.

Every church I know of could fill its chairs at least thirty times over with the people who passed through their doors and are now sitting home offended over one thing or another.

To put the icing on the cake, there are Christians that think, "If everyone just believed like me and my church believes, God would be happy."

First of all, God is not unhappy. He's doing quite well. And second, the last thing we all need is more believers that are meaner than a one-eyed snake, and won't talk to other people because they think of themselves as spiritually superior.

Is it possible that not walking in unity with other believers could be the single largest obstacle in our whole Christian walk?

When you look closely at what Paul writes to the Corinthians, God thinks that unity is very important.

"But I urge you, believers, by the name of our

> Lord Jesus Christ, that all of you be in full
> agreement in what you say, and that there
> be no divisions or factions among you, but
> that you be perfectly united in your way of
> thinking and in your judgment [about matters
> of the faith]" (1 Corinthians 1:10 AMP).

We see that the book of Colossians also emphasizes the importance of "*a perfect bond of unity, bearing graciously with one another, and willingly forgiving each other if one has a cause for complaint against another; just as the Lord has forgiven you, so should you forgive. Beyond all these things put on and wrap yourselves in* [unselfish] *love, which is the perfect bond of unity* [for everything is bound together in agreement when each one seeks the best for others]" (Colossians 3:13-14 AMP).

In the book of John, Jesus said that our unity proves that God the Father sent Jesus as proof of the Father's love.

> "*I am in them and you are in me. May they
> experience such perfect unity that the world
> will know that you sent me and that you love
> them as much as you love me*" (John 17:23
> NLT).

The Missing Link

We live in a day when churches are run like businesses; people are a commodity, and their franchises extend into new areas where their products are sold daily.

Most churches, and even their members, view other churches and their members as "the competition."

In our quest to conquer new territories and add new people to our numbers, new members become a sought-after commodity that keeps the wheels of progress rolling.

If the truth were known, competition among churches is just as strong as the competition in the secular marketplace. One church losing a good number of their members to another church causes a deep hurt between the two churches. This is something that no one talks about, but we all know it's true. If there's one thing that churches and their respective members do not have, it's unity.

Every so often, in every city, a pastor will put out a clarion call for a unity meeting among churches. Most churches will not even respond to the invitation, some, because the meeting was not their idea or under their leadership. The ones that do respond really try to make the effort towards unity. It is always an awkward event with all the distrust from the hurts of the past.

Most believers don't have a screaming idea about how important unity is to God and how much it grieves Him that we don't have it. Unity is as elusive as Bigfoot; everyone has heard of it, but who can ever say they've actually seen the real thing, or agree about what it looks like?

At our first few revivals, our five Southeast Louisiana Revival pastors stood in front of the auditorium, and instead of each of us having equal time to share, we each passed the microphone on to the next pastor. As each of us preferred the other, and the presence of the Holy Spirit was so strong, a couple of us just thanked God for His presence, and I believe I was the one crying.

Later, one of our church members said, "To see pastors in such unity! In all my life I've never seen such a miracle; it was better than if I had seen someone raised from the dead!"

That night the Holy Spirit moved in power, healing the sick and changing lives like I have never seen in thirty years of ministry!

Little Clubs or Great Unity

When you ask someone about their relationship with the Lord, they usually respond with something about the particular denomination or religion they belong to.

As we all know, the denomination or religion you belong to speaks loud and clear about the doctrines you believe in - well, at least the doctrines that you are *supposed* to believe in. This is so common that no one thinks twice about it.

Let's take a minute to explore the implications.

Any denomination or religious group became what it is because of the doctrines it accepted as truth, versus the doctrines it rejected as being false or less important.

I'm sure many of us have had conversations with people, and said something that could potentially ruffle religious feathers. My experience has been that, when I did ruffle feathers, the other person would respond, "Well I'm a Catholic," or "I'm a Presbyterian," or "I'm Baptist." It's as if they pulled out their **"*diplomatic immunity card,*"** so they could shut down the conversation. What they were really saying was, "I may not be sure of what I believe, but I still don't want you to challenge it."

Let's follow this train of thought.

Have you ever thought about which group Jesus would belong to if He were alive on the earth today? We tend to believe that surely He would be a committed member of the denomination that we belong to.

I have had people tell me all the time that they are a faithful Episcopalian, or a faithful Catholic, or a faithful Baptist, but suggest that they don't really believe *everything* their denomination puts forward. My question is, why would you belong to it if you disagree with some of their major views on scripture? And further, why allow a denominational label to be a point of contention with other believers in Christ?

What a person believes speaks loud and clear about who he or she really is as a person and where that person is going in this life and into eternity.

In his letter to the Romans, Paul pointed out that what you believe means everything:

> "*For it is by believing in your heart that you are made right with God, and it is by openly declaring your faith that you are saved*" (Romans 10:10 NLT).

To further complicate matters, many people belong to their particular denomination or religion **because they were born into it**.

That means that many of them never made a real choice to belong to it based on what they believe. Then because of "the pride of man," they believe the same way they did when they were children, as if to say, *my little club is better than your little club.*

The truth is that nobody's little club is better than anyone else's club. Our little club has never been, nor will it ever be, the standard for truth.

Divisions within the body of Christ are the result of man's interpretation of the ultimate truth, the Word of God. I believe that it's safe to say that God does not care one bit – no, not even one *little* bit - about our little clubs. He cares about *us*!

If God favored one of our little clubs over another, He would have endorsed one of them by now, and He hasn't!

2 Timothy 3:16 clarifies, "*All Scripture is inspired by God and is useful to teach us what is true and to make us realize what is wrong in our lives. It corrects us when we are wrong and teaches us to*

do what is right." NLT

When God's Word becomes the final authority in our lives and it supersedes what we or anyone else thinks or says, we become real disciples of Christ rather than members of a religion.

You are probably wondering, "So what do all the little clubs have to do with unity or lack of it if we are faithful to them?"

Well, I'm glad to address that. All the little clubs were never God's intention, and they actually hinder us by the separation of, and conflict over, doctrines. A search of the scriptures makes it clear that God wants us to have unity among ourselves.

Great Unity

Let's take a look at what God originally intended for the Church. To do that, we have to look at the birth of the Church in the second chapter of Acts.

> "*When the Day of Pentecost had fully come, they were all **with one accord** in one place. And suddenly there came a sound from Heaven, as of a rushing mighty wind, and it filled the whole house where they were sitting*" (Acts 2:1-2 NKJV).

When the Bible uses the word, "accord," it is translated from the Greek word for "unity." As we look up "unity" in Webster's dictionary, it is defined as "oneness" or "a condition of harmony or accord." This is what God originally intended for His people and His Church, that we would live in unity.

We could all agree that the Holy Spirit thrives in an atmosphere of love, peace, and unity. That being true, the opposite is also true. Where there is hatred, anger, division, and disunity, there will be no move of the Holy Spirit at all!

Mark 3:25 makes this clear: "*And if a house is divided against itself, that house cannot stand*" (NKJV).

The opposite of unity is division. Division destroys churches, marriages, business ventures, friendships, and anything it touches.

Before we look at what God's Word says about unity, let's explore division and disunity a little further. Somebody needs to hear this:

> "*In the last days there will be scoffers... following after their own ungodly passions. It is these who are [agitators]... causing divisions...worldly-minded people*" (Jude 1:18-19 AMP).

And if I may amplify the Amplified version of the Bible, these scoffers are secular, unspiritual, carnal, merely sensual, unsaved, and devoid of the Spirit.

I believe that if we look closely at this problem in the church, we will see that the root of division is judging others. As we read the following scripture carefully we can see the far-reaching implications:

"Judge not, that you be not judged. For with what judgment you judge, you will be judged; and with the measure you use, it will be measured back to you" (Matthew 7:1-2 NKJV).

According to this, when we judge, we ourselves come under the judgment of God. It's a warning that we would do well to take seriously.

The great question before us now is, who is able to accomplish the work that has been set before them while they are unknowingly under the judgment of God?

Probably the worst form of judging is not when we judge the actions, but the characteristics and the differences of other people. Let me take it a step further: some people look at the uniqueness of others and criticize it, when we should actually accept and enjoy their uniqueness, viewing it as the way the Potter made the vessel.

Think about a football team. If everybody was a quarterback, who would catch the ball and who would block the receiver?

What would happen if you had a whole team of kickers? There would just be a bunch of smaller guys running around getting hurt!

A great team is made up of people who have various giftings and talents working together for the same goal and purpose.

Some people want to sit around criticizing, and

judging everyone for not being just like them, which does nothing but make everyone miserable. There are, however, some who are able to accept and even celebrate the differences and uniqueness of others.

The ball is in our court. We alone decide whether we will judge the differences of others or celebrate them.

The apostle Paul wrote this to the church in Rome, "*Now I urge you, brethren, note those who cause divisions and offenses, contrary to the doctrine which you learned, and avoid them*" (Romans 16:17 NKJV).

When Paul spoke about people who cause divisions, he was talking about people who cause disunity. There are certain people in life that are negative about everything; they usually gossip and cause great harm to others. God's Word says that gossip is one of the seven things that He hates (Proverbs 6:16), and all gossip stems from judging others.

People say it's not gossip if it's true. Well, that's a lie. People who gossip usually haven't gotten any of their gossip verified before defiling themselves or others with their words.

When people gossip – even if the report is factually true – it's the same as stabbing the person you are gossiping about with a knife.

This is a brutal analogy, but it's true.

Paul wrote in Romans 16:17 that we should avoid those who cause division.

There are times when we, as Christians, hear people judging others, gossiping, and just causing divisions.

Imagine the results if we just had the guts to tell them nicely, "Hey, I really don't want to hear it."

That person is not here to defend himself. It's wrong. God hates it and you need to stop it.

It would be bold, but we would really be helping them to see the light; not to mention that we would be helping the people who are the objects of their ridicule.

It's a great time to be reminded that,

A Miracle for Katy

Katy attends Pastor Bill's church in Kenner, Louisiana. On the very first night of our revival baptisms, one of the first people to get in the water was Katy, whom we've known personally for many years. Katy and her former husband are in their early eighties; they were divorced many years ago, but never remarried. When Katy got into the water, she said that Jesus spoke to her and said, "You cannot come to Heaven and be with me until you get things right with your former husband." She knew just what Jesus was talking about. She called her husband and asked his forgiveness. She told him that he was not

- continued -

"Blessed be the peacemakers: for they shall be

called the children of God" (Matthew 5:9 KJV).

Sometimes being a peacemaker requires boldness enough to say, "Let's just stop all that!"

Katy continued:

responsible for their divorce, saying "I failed to meet your needs like a man needs his needs met. It was my fault, not yours."

Her husband said, "Okay, but, at our age, I really don't want to go back together."

She said, "I wasn't wanting to go back with you; I just wanted to make things right."

He said, "Listen, don't ever worry about a thing. I'm going to take care of you for the rest of your life."

Hey, come on, now! That's what I call REVIVAL!

There are many scriptures that speak about the blessings of God. In particular, Psalm 133:1 says it's a good thing when brothers dwell in unity. That verse flows into verse three where God **commands** the blessing.

> "*Behold, how good and how pleasant it is for brethren to dwell together in unity! It is like the precious oil upon the head, running down on the beard, the beard of Aaron, running*

down on the edge of his garments. It is like the dew of Hermon, descending upon the mountains of Zion; for there the Lord commanded the blessing—life forevermore" (Psalm 133:1-3 NKJV).

How tremendous is that!

Because of coming into unity, God actually commands a blessing upon us!

Just the other day, at one of our revival meetings, I addressed the crowd about the subject of unity. I said that this whole revival that has already touched so many lives was conceived in prayer, but it was birthed in unity.

The real story is that I had a real problem with the former pastor of our church. I remember a time when I told the Lord, "I don't like some of the things he did," and the Lord told me, "Yes, and I don't like some of the things you did."

Ok, ok, so let's just say that there was an offense there, but I made it right! We reconciled the offense and when we began Southeast Louisiana Revival, I asked that pastor to come be part of our revival group. I remember so clearly telling him, "We need you; without you this whole thing will not work."

God had shown me that he and I, in unity, would be greatly used by Him. Today, he and I are close friends and he preaches at our revival meetings. Now tell me, is that God, or what?

Questions for Reflection:

1. Who is it in my life that I have an unresolved conflict with?

2. Is it possible that this unresolved conflict has hindered my life and or ministry?

3. What is stopping me from making this right today?

Chapter 9

Thy Kingdom, My Kingdom. Whose Kingdom is it, Anyway?

In the previous chapter, we pinpointed what may possibly be the greatest hindrance to the gospel - disunity among all believers.

If, in fact, this is accurate, let's dig a little deeper. I believe that it is easy for us to agree with the main causes for our lack of unity: our little clubs, our pet doctrines, judging others, and, of course, pride. But let's see if we can find the root cause.

Ok, let's fasten our seatbelts again and prepare to go places where few dare to go. Here we go!

There are many people who preach the gospel, but very few preach the gospel that Jesus preached.

You might be saying that this is a very brash statement. Instead of being offended by it and rejecting it, let's do some investigating.

Most religions teach that you will go to Heaven because you are part of their group. Scripture does not support that idea. In fact, the Bible simply says that God loves us, and if we believe in Christ as Savior and receive Him, we become children of God.

> "*For God so loved the world that He gave His only begotten Son, that whoever believes in Him should not perish but have everlasting life*" (John 3:16 NKJV).

In agreement with this thought, John 1:12 says, "*But as many as received Him, to them He gave the right to become children of God, to those who believe in His name*" (NKJV).

Simply put, we receive salvation by grace, through Jesus Christ who died for us on the cross.

Ephesians 2:8-10 says that "*God saved you by His grace when you believed. And you can't take credit for this; it is a gift from God. For we are his workmanship, created in Christ Jesus for good works, which God prepared before that we would walk in them.*" NLT

The New Living Translation says it in a unique way: "*Salvation is not a reward for the good things we have done, so none of us can boast about it. For we are God's masterpiece. He has created us anew in Christ Jesus, so we can do the good things he planned for us long ago.*"

The words "salvation" or "saved" are found a total

Danielle

My name is Danielle and I am thirty-four. I have dealt with severe depression and suicidal thoughts since I was thirteen. On good days I just wasn't happy. On bad days I felt alone, unloved, and worthless. I tried to kill myself several times, and every night I would pray that the Lord would let me die in my sleep. Then in the morning I would ask why I was still here. I never went to the doctor or sought help because I saw it as a defect in myself and chose to deal with it on my own. When the church started having baptism revivals, I was skeptical. But after hearing about it so much, I decided I would go. I went to the House on the Rock, but Cornerstone, the church across the street was leading it. During the whole service I fought with myself about whether to get baptized.

CONTINUED NEXT PAGE

of ninety-three times in the New Testament, depending on which version you use. The word "kingdom," however, is used many more times, as many as 162 times in the New Testament alone.

Now, why is that so important?

It's very simple. Even though Jesus said that we must be saved, He preached over and over about the Kingdom. This is why I say that many people preach the gospel, but few preach the gospel that Jesus preached!

First of all, God is King; He is not a president. He

Danielle CONTINUED

While I was in line to be baptized, I kept thinking about leaving. I got to the bottom of the steps before you get into the pool, and someone asked what I came for. I told them I want all of God. As they were praying for me, the man leaned over and whispered in my ear that God had shown him I was wearing a mask, that I smile and act like I'm happy, but I'm really broken and hurting inside. He said, once I come out of the water, I'll really be happy. I was shocked how he knew my deepest secret. Later, a friend asked me how I was doing. And I said, "I'm fine," but I quickly realized I was actually happy. For twenty-one years I tried not to think about how I felt because it always made it worse. But the mask is gone and I have a peace that I never knew was possible. God met me in the water that night and healed me.

was not elected, and He will never need to be re-elected.

> "*The Lord has established His throne in the heavens, and His sovereignty rules over all commandments, obeying the voice of His Word! Bless the Lord, all you His hosts, you who serve Him and do His will*" (Psalm 103:19-21 AMP).

When a kingdom extends its territory, people living in the new colony function under the rule of the king. When England, France, and Spain started colonies in the New World, those colonies not only functioned under their respective kingdoms, but they actually took on their cultures, too.

It's difficult for us, as Americans, to understand a king and a kingdom, because we were raised in a democratic society. Basically, we Americans question everything; we think for ourselves, and honestly, we don't appreciate anyone telling us what to do. Conversely, those who were raised in a kingdom understand that a king is the sovereign authority, and the people are subjects of the king.

For example, if you lived in an English colony, you spoke English, drank hot tea, and lived in buildings that reflected English architecture.

When God created the earth, He also created man to have dominion over the earth. As we all know, in the garden, Adam lost his dominion to another kingdom: the kingdom of darkness.

John the Baptist prepared the way for Jesus with the words, "*Repent, for the Kingdom of Heaven is at hand*" (Matthew 3:2 NKJV).

When Jesus began His ministry, these were His opening words, "*Repent, for the Kingdom of Heaven is at hand*" (Matthew 4:17 NKJV)

In our day, seldom - if ever - will you hear the word "repent" used in a sermon, and most of us have never heard a sermon on the Kingdom.

Jesus walked on the beach at the Sea of Galilee,

where He met Peter, Andrew, James, and John. They had no idea that they had just met Christ, the Messiah, the Holy Lamb of God. They were the first of the disciples, and this was the beginning of their ministry.

Matthew 4:23 says, *"And Jesus went about all Galilee, teaching in their synagogues, preaching the gospel of the Kingdom, and healing all kinds of sickness and all kinds of disease among the people."* NKJV

The message of the Kingdom was the central theme of Jesus' ministry. It was so important that, near the end of His ministry, He instructed His disciples to continue preaching the Kingdom:

> *"And this gospel of the Kingdom will be preached in all the world as a witness to all the nations, and then the end will come"* (Matthew 24:14 NKJV).

The Kingdom of Heaven vs The Kingdom of God

Bible scholars have had many lengthy - and I'm sure, heated - debates over the different kingdoms mentioned in God's Word.

In the Old Testament, there are mentions of many different kingdoms of men. And we know, also, that there is the kingdom of darkness.

Our focus will be on the Kingdom of Heaven and the Kingdom of God.

Together, we find these two kingdoms mentioned approximately 150 times in scripture, again, depending on the translation used. However, the real question is, how are the two kingdoms different?

In Matthew 6:25-32, Jesus is telling His listeners not to worry about food or clothing; He said that if your heavenly Father can take care of the flowers of the fields and the birds of the air, He can surely take care of you. He said your heavenly Father already knows your needs! Then, in verse 33, in only nineteen words, Jesus gives us the ultimate prescription to all worry and anxiety:

> *"But seek first the Kingdom of God and His righteousness, and all these things shall be added to you"* (Matthew 6:33 NKJV).

Here, we see that the Kingdom of God is not a place you go to. That term means, through your obedience, God's Word is working in your life! It means when you obey His commands, one way or another, when you live a life that is pleasing to God, everything will work out!

In Matthew, chapter nineteen, there was a rich young ruler that wanted to have the assurance of eternal salvation. After dialoguing with the young man, Jesus told him to sell all he had and to give to the poor. This story in no way means that every wealthy person needs to sell all their possessions. However, in this case the young man's many

possessions were the root of his problems. This is

why Jesus told him to sell his possessions and give to the poor and he would have treasure in Heaven.

> *"But when the young man heard that saying, he went away sorrowful, for he had great possessions. Then Jesus said to His disciples, 'Assuredly, I say to you that it is hard for a rich man to enter the Kingdom of Heaven. And again I say to you, it is easier for a camel to go through the eye of a needle than for a rich man to enter the Kingdom of God'"* (Matthew 19:22 NKJV).

The terms, "Kingdom of Heaven" and "Kingdom of God" are both used in the same story. Jesus told the rich young ruler that it would be hard for him to enter the Kingdom of Heaven (referring to eternity in Heaven) because of his present standing in the Kingdom of God.

In other words, "his walk didn't line up with his talk." This lines up with all of scripture; God expects us to obey His Word.

Generally, we see in scripture that the term, Kingdom of God, is used to define the spiritual realm wherein a person lives and walks out the righteousness of God in the earth.

Generally, we see in scripture that the term, Kingdom of Heaven, is used to describe the place where God lives in Heaven, where we will one day be with Him.

It is a widely accepted Bible doctrine that those

who died before the resurrection of Christ went to a place called Abraham's bosom or Paradise. After Jesus' death on the cross, He took back the keys to death, hell and the grave. When Jesus began his ministry with the words, "*Repent, for the Kingdom of Heaven is at hand*," He was saying that Heaven's doors will soon be open and the key to enter is repentance.

Therefore, repentance is the key to both the Kingdom of God and the Kingdom of Heaven!.

Now that we have laid some basic groundwork for the Kingdom, let's move on. If, in fact, the previous part of this chapter is accurate - and I believe that it is - where does that leave us all?

For those of us who claim to be followers of Christ, if we are saved and headed for the Kingdom of Heaven, is the Kingdom of God actively working in our lives?

Are we really kingdom-minded?

We need to face the truth that we can be saved, but at the same time, jealous and envious of others and how God is using them. Can we be saved – and. yes, even Spirit-filled - but at the same time, solely concerned with building only "our kingdom"?

I was listening to a minister one day as he used the term, kingdom, very liberally, but, at the same time, his actions seemed to stipulate, "as long as *I'm* in charge."

Is it possible that the previously mentioned lack of

unity among believers - including church leaders as a whole - is a result of a basic lack of kingdom-mindedness? When a person is kingdom-minded, it changes the way he relates to and responds to others.

Characteristics of Kingdom-Minded People

- They know that prayer brings results, not just for their own efforts or purposes.

- They are never in competition with other churches or church members.

- They are never in fear of losing what was given to them by God.

- They care about what God is doing everywhere, not just in their area.

- They are not afraid of giving opportunity to others.

- They are not afraid that another church has more members than theirs.

- They are not afraid of who gets the credit.

- They can rejoice with others when God uses them and blesses them.

This is a chapter that leaves us at no other place than the place of self evaluation. If Jesus preached that repentance would lead us into the Kingdom of Heaven, He intended that same repentance to lead us into a life where the Kingdom of God is working more deeply in our lives.

We need the Kingdom of God affecting the way we look at others, relate to others and respond to others.

A Miracle for Debbie

Debbie, from Life House Church in Reserve, Louisiana, was diagnosed with the early stages of colon cancer.

She and her husband Ray decided not to rush into cancer treatment. Ray said they believed that, "we had a treatment plan of our own: Jesus!

"We prayed and believed the Lord would heal her, and I believe we had a breakthrough one night at St. James Community Church."

Let Ray tell you in his own words.

"That night, at a revival, she and I got baptized, praying for the cancer to be gone. Well, she just finished the follow-up test and the doctor just came in and gave me the news that we were expecting. She is cancer-free! Yes, the Lord heard our cries and healed her.

"Jesus is our Healer, and is still doing miracles today!"

Questions for Reflection:

1. Am I kingdom-minded?

2. Can I - right now - repent of the fears and insecurities that led me to be the king of my own kingdom?

3. Can I humbly ask God to be the King of my life?

Chapter 10

Jesus Said to Make Disciples, But How Do You Do It?

Jesus commanded his followers to go into all the world, to make disciples, to baptize them and to teach them to follow Him.

But who do you ever see making a disciple?

Like me, you may have asked the question, "Was this command just for His *first* disciples?"

If that were the case, Christianity would not exist today.

Some might question that conclusion, wondering, how could that possibly be? Maybe Jesus meant this just for church leaders to obey.

If we say that the Great Commission isn't for us today, then maybe God's grace, His mercy, and His healing power aren't for today. But just as God commands that we baptize, He has commanded us to make disciples. Let's read it:

"Go therefore and make disciples of all the nations, baptizing them in the name of the Father and of the Son and of the Holy Spirit, teaching them to observe all things that I have commanded you; and lo, I am with you always, even to the end of the age. Amen" (Matthew 28:19-20 NKJV).

The Great Commission tells us to make disciples, but how many of us have ever made a disciple? And did someone actually take the time to disciple you?

On December 31, 1991, the former Soviet Union collapsed. For the past seventy years, the Russian people had been taught that there was no God; this resulted in a great spiritual vacuum.

For any minister that wanted to do great things for God, this collapse was the opportunity of a lifetime, because Russian people were very hungry for God. By the end of the next year, Rinalda and I had sold almost everything we owned and relocated in Ivanova, Russia. Within another six months, we were ministering in the small city of Furmanov.

Missionaries from our organization were literally some of the first missionaries on the ground. Most cities had no Christian church at all. With all the large, beautiful cities where we could have planted a church, we were led to this very small city called Furmanov. The people there had never seen an American before.

We rented a large auditorium in the city and held a

three-night Christian music festival. At the end of the third night, we made an announcement for everyone to come back on Sunday morning, because we would be holding church services in the auditorium.

Our first service was attended by 500 people, and our worship team was a rock and roll band that had been saved for less than a few months.

When we made the decision to plant a church in Furmanov, we had no idea that we were being totally led by the Holy Spirit. Most of our church was made up of young people that were hungry to learn about Jesus. At this time we held leadership classes for, sometimes, seventy to eighty young church members.

My dear friend and fellow missionary, Mark Leonard, started a Bible college in the neighboring city of Ivanova. That first year, I was one of the teachers in the Ivanova Ministry Training Institute, and many of the students were young people from the Furmanov church.

The Day the Light Came On

One day, between classes, I had a conversation with Dr. Jerry King, a visiting Bible college professor. Little did I know that this was a conversation that would change the course of my life.

He said, "Larry, aren't a lot of these young people from your church?"

Shanna Barberio

On March 13, I had the honor of being a "dunker" in the pool during a baptism service. What a powerful night! At the end of a night of marinating in revival waters, Pastor Mervin prayed over me before it was my turn to take a plunge. I believe he was directed by God to pray that I would write a song about that night. The next morning I sat at home on my keyboard like I normally do and that prayer came to mind. So I started putting words to a melody and a complete song was written in about an hour! That's not normal for me. I'm still working on songs that are two years old. The following week I wrote two more songs. Since then I've written poems and songs, and I am about to finish two books on prayer and worship! Praise God! When you combine a faith-filled prayer and revival fire, gifts are unlocked and activated.

I proudly said, "Yes, they sure are!"

Then Dr. King said, "So how do you plan on discipling them?"

I told him, "Well, we have them in a discipleship class."

Again he asked, "So Larry, how do you plan on discipling them?"

Again I said, "I told you, we have them in a discipleship class."

Then a third time, he asked, "So Larry, how do you plan on discipling them?"

By this time I was a little aggravated with him and I laughingly said,

"I guess you didn't hear me. I told you twice that I have them in a discipleship class."

At that moment he turned to me and said, "You don't have a clue about what you are doing, do you?"

Obviously, there was a little tension in the air, so I said, "Well then, tell me how should I disciple them?"

He said Jesus didn't teach a class and he didn't use curriculum. He lived with them, ate with them, answered their questions, showed them how it was done, and he gave them opportunity.

I remember thinking that I had never heard anything like this. It was as if a light came on, and it was something that I would remember for the rest of my life.

Some of Our First Disciples

At that time, we were having a small group in our apartment in Furmanov. You have to realize, the bottom had fallen out of the Russian economy and food was scarce. But as missionaries, we had the means to buy food. One thing we all have in common is that we all have a stomach.

In Russia, people were used to eating crepes, but they had never seen American pancakes. Rinalda is an incredible cook, and she soon became a celebrity, making thousands of pancakes for hungry young Russians in our small group.

That small group lasted a year and a half. We taught the whole time on the heart, and how to have a heart after God. We fed them, loved them and we played games. I do believe that some of these kids had never played games before.

I remember one night that one of our interpreters pointed out one of the young men with a disheveled look. She said, "He doesn't need to be here; he's only here for the food."

I remember telling her, "If he's just here for the food, that's ok. He'll find more than food here."

There was an older couple that lived in a village on the edge of Furmanov. Under communism, they had a very small group of believers that secretly met in their home. Each time they met, they closed the curtains and quietly worshiped the Lord. For years they prayed and asked the Lord to bring real Christianity to their country, and for a church to be established in Furmanov.

It turned out that this couple had a prodigal son. This young man ended up not only in our church, but in my small group, and a student in the Bible college where I taught. That same young man, whose name is Volodia, turned out to be the one that was identified as being in my small group just for the food!

God always answers our prayers in ways we would never expect.

At this same time in Furmanov we had a youth

pastor named Mervin Strother. Mervin was a young man that we had poured our life into back in the States. Now with Mervin on our Furmanov team, he was with us during our whole ministry.

When the young Russians were not at my apartment, they were staying at Mervin's apartment. Our young Russian worship leader, Sasha, actually lived with him. All this continuous love, fellowship, and connection led to real discipleship that took place in Furmanov.

When we left Furmanov to plant a church in another city, it was Volodia that became the pastor of the Furmanov church. Today, he pastors in another city in Russia. Mervin Strother pastors a church in Amite, Louisiana, and is one of our Southeast Louisiana Revival pastors. Sasha is a worship leader in Irkutsk, Siberia. A total of seven ministers came out of that small group in the city of Furmanov, and we learned the secret of making disciples

Making Disciples

Fast forwarding a number of years when we pastored another church, a young couple visited one Sunday morning and, believe me, they were "one hot mess!" They both had children from previous relationships, and brought with them serious drug and pornography issues. They really loved each other, were gloriously saved, and they got married in our church.

Soon after we met them, it was as if the Lord tapped me on the shoulder and said, "Disciple them."

This is how we did it.

I invited the couple to come over for dinner with their children. We had a nice dinner and then played board games. This was something that was totally foreign to them. It was like WOW! This is how families have fun!

At the end of the evening, as they were leaving, I said, "Hey guys, I want you to come back next week and let's have dinner again!"

They said, "Sure, sounds great!"

The next week, we had dinner and games again, and at the end of the evening I said, "Hey, come back next week."

And they said, "Sure!"

The following week, we had a great dinner with games and fellowship. At the end of the evening, when I invited them back, the husband asked, "Hey, what's going on around here?"

I explained that we saw that God had a great plan for their lives together. I added that we believed in them and we wanted to make an investment of time into their lives.

They looked at each other, looked at us, and simply said, "Ok."

Our Sunday evening meetings lasted nearly two years. During that time, we played games and just talked about life and raising children.

The Breaking Point

One evening, about six months after we had started meeting with them, they were late. This hadn't happened before, so I knew something was wrong.

When I called them, I could get neither of them on the phone. I believed that the Lord wanted me to go to their home, so off I went. When I arrived there, they were reluctant to let me in, but when I entered the house, I simply asked them, "How could you possibly be late for dinner when we have dinner on the table?"

Without getting into detail, let me just say that she was locked in the bathroom, and he was bouncing off the walls in drug-induced craziness. And a gun was in the mix, for added drama.

I told them to ditch the gun and the drugs, and that we would have dinner waiting for them the next week at the usual time.

"Don't be late," I added.

That was a breaking point in their recovery and it never happened again!

When the next week rolled around, they were there at our home and our evenings together were back on track.

We never mentioned that dark night that they went through.

Great Success

One evening they were at our home, and we were barbecuing. I simply told the husband that we really enjoyed investing into their lives, and that the only thing we wanted from them in return is that, one day, they would do this for other couples.

He looked at me and said, "I will, I promise I will."

We never did tell them that we were discipling them. Nor did we ever have a Bible study. We just loved them and we talked about what it was like for us, serving God throughout our lives.

Today, this couple is still in church. They have a stable marriage, they are great parents, and they are a vital part of their church. And they have a great future ahead of them.

I have no doubt that they will accomplish great things for the Kingdom, and that they will have a passion for making disciples.

God has already invested so much in each of us; He has been with us through the hard times and has pulled us through our darkest hours. The truth is that we already have what others need. We just need to make a decision to invest in the lives of others.

A Miracle for Renee

For twelve years, Renee, from Life House Church in Reserve, Louisiana, struggled with stomach issues. She would have excruciating abdominal pain, nausea, vomiting, and diarrhea lasting days, weeks and sometimes even months. She was taking five to seven pills a day to keep her pain level tolerable.

Renee had a colonoscopy and biopsy done, and it came back that she had a rare disease called Eosinophilic Colitis. She had lost about twenty pounds and had been eating only canned soup for months.

She entered the baptism waters determined to receive healing. The day after being baptized, she felt a burning in her stomach, and by the third day, she was eating Popeye's fried chicken and was off her medications.

She said, "Jesus is amazing and is in the business of healing people, if you will just come expecting!!!"

What a phenomenal testimony!

Questions for Reflection:

1. Am I willing to make disciples?

2. Am I willing to start now?

Chapter 11

Words

If you have read this far, you are about to see the power of words, and the effect they have on those who hear them. When revival comes to a person's life, one thing it does is, it opens his or her eyes to the spiritual realm.

Everything we do, and especially what we speak, carries over into eternity.

A Negative World

The news networks traverse the globe just to be at ground zero in hopes of reporting the latest catastrophe. We all know that the worse the pain, and the greater the suffering, the more it is sensationalized in the news.

For the most part, politicians are congenial to their respective counterparts until election time. Then it becomes a free-for-all, as they tell how bad it would be if the opposition were elected. From the picture they paint, if we vote for their opponent, it will be as if we elected Adolf Hitler. Then we are left with the conjured-up visions of us all being carted away to concentration camps.

The truth is, we live in a negative world!

However, isn't it a breath of fresh air when we run across a person who is positive and just has that uncompromising joy of the Lord? The Bible says it like this, "*The joy of the Lord is your strength*" (Nehemiah 8:10 NKJV).

Being happy, joyful and positive is a strength that every believer can have. The kink in the chain is our carnal nature; it's the flaw that enables a believer to still be negative.

The Power of Words

Our words carry power, and we have the God-given ability to bless or curse our own lives and the lives of others. Every day, with the words of our mouths, we curse or bless our marriage, children, family, friends, finances, and future.

In light of this, we need to ask ourselves, "What is the attitude that I have about myself and other people? Is it positive or negative?"

Words are so powerful that, in the beginning, when there was nothing - think about it, when nothing at all existed - God said, "*Let there be light!*" (Genesis 1:3 NKJV).

Though nothing existed, creation began with four words. Those four words already existed in the heart of God, but nothing happened until those four words were spoken.

Consider the power in this proclamation: when God said, "*Let us make man - someone like ourselves, to be the master of all life upon the earth and in the skies and in the seas*" (Genesis 1:26 TLB).

First of all, when God's Word says, "*Let us make man - someone like ourselves...*," that means that we were created to have not only the capacity for love, reason, and choice, but, in addition, we were created to carry the Spirit of God!

When we believe, He comes to live inside of us!

Second, when God said, "*...to be the master of all life upon the earth and in the skies and in the seas*," He meant that you were divinely made with a purpose and a destiny.

You did not originate from slime that crawled up on a rock out of the sea, and your ancestor was not a monkey.

We were uniquely made by God, and He created us so that we would love Him by our own free will. We have the power of choice, which is expressed in words. It is with words that we worship God, express our love, and bless Him and others.

Words are powerful!

Words Direct our Lives

Your words will build and strengthen your life, or they will weaken it and tear it down.

Jesus said this about the power of words, "*For assuredly, I say to you, whoever says to this mountain, 'Be removed and be cast into the sea,' and does not doubt in his heart, but believes that those things he says will be done, he will have whatever he says"* (Mark 11:23 NKJV).

When Jesus spoke those words, the mountain He was speaking about was not a literal mountain; He was and is speaking about the mountain-sized problems, obstacles, and situations that we encounter in life!

The average person complains about his or her problems. My question is, Who wants to be average?

You did not originate from slime that crawled up on a rock out of the sea, and your ancestor was not a monkey.

In the Old Testament, God delivered His people out of Egyptian bondage and appointed Moses to lead them to the Promised Land, flowing with milk and honey. It was so bountiful that two men had to use a pole to carry one cluster of grapes! The down-side was, giants occupied the land. Wow, that's scary!

Look at what took place when twelve men returned who were sent to spy out the bountiful land:

"As for the men whom Moses sent to spy out the land, and who returned and made all the congregation murmur and complain against him by bringing back a bad report concerning the land,

*even those [ten] men who brought back the very
bad report of the land died by a plague before the
Lord. But Joshua the son of Nun and Caleb the son
of Jephunneh remained alive out of those men who
went to spy out the land"* (Numbers 14:36-38
AMP).

There may be no greater example of what can
happen when we speak negatively. The ten who
slandered the land not only failed to enter the land,
they died of a plague. The two who spoke
positively about the land entered it, enjoyed the
land, and possessed it.

As a pastor, I'd have to say that things haven't
changed much. In my dealings with people, I'd say
that this Old Testament account pretty accurately
portrays the percentages that exist in today's
population. Out of any group of twelve random
people, maybe I would find two who would be truly
positive.

We have the power to choose to possess godly
character, and godly character is positive. What the
ten spies missed is this: if God brought them to the
Promised Land and said it was theirs, what did it
matter if there were giants in the land?

Think about it, God had brought ten plagues upon
Egypt to set His people free. Then when the
Egyptian army chased after God's people, God
drowned the entire army in the sea, and His people
crossed on dry land. God did those great miracles,
and more! So why would the Israelites care about a

few giants?

The very same thing is true for us.

Sometimes we need to stop and take an inventory of all that God has brought us through, rescued us from, and blessed us with. When we look at all that, the giant that stands before us now begins to look pretty small!

No matter what God gives you, there will be problems to solve and maintenance to be done.

When God gives you a marriage or children, a job,

a career, a business, or relationships, they need upkeep.

My wife and I like to say marriage is like a garden; you reap what you plant in your garden or marriage. Plant in your marriage what you want to harvest, like mercy, forgiveness, and kindness. Then when you are in need, you will find in your marriage what you have planted - or failed to plant.

Words Bring Life or Death

God's Word says it like this, "*Death and life are in the power of the tongue*" (Proverbs 18:21 NKJV).

You talk down, you will go down.

You talk defeat, you will be defeated.

You talk lack, you will have lack.

You talk depression, you will be depressed.

You talk supernatural, you will see the supernatural.

You talk good, you will see good.

You talk blessing, you will be blessed.

Have you ever heard of a football coach giving a pregame speech about off season depression? Of course not! A great football coach gives a pregame victory speech!

This is not mind over matter; this is the truth of the Word of God. We just need to agree with what God already says about us. God says that we are loved, that we are healed, and that we are whole. In fact, God's children are His prized possession.

Words are more powerful than we can imagine. Just imagine the power behind the words, "I do."

Just imagine the power behind the words, "Lord, I repent, and I ask you to come into my life."

When people are born again, they become new creations. Their spirits come alive in Christ; they are now speaking spirits, with the power to declare and proclaim God's Word, His goodness, and His direction in their lives.

With the words of our mouths, we can actually change the atmosphere and bring peace to a situation. On one hand, we have the power to use words to bring blessing to a person's life; on the other, we can curse them. It is far better to bless someone with our words, such as, "I believe in you.

I appreciate you. I'm going to take care of you. I love you!"

When people choose to use words to curse, friendships are ended, families are separated, couples are divorced, lives are torn apart.

With words, it's possible for lives to be healed, but someone has to be big enough to utter the words, "I'm sorry. Please forgive me."

I was raised in a good family. My parents didn't have a close walk with the Lord; like most parents, they did the best they could. In the first grade, I remember making good grades and enjoying school, but when I entered the second grade, I started having great difficulty, especially with reading.

By the time I entered the third grade, my studies were so bad that I failed the third grade. In those days, they were not testing for learning disabilities, and no one had a clue that was my problem. My dad was so frustrated, he had no idea what to do with me. I remember so clearly him bending over, and shouting at me over and over, "What is wrong with you?"

As a little kid, I had no idea what was wrong with me, but I grew up convinced that something was definitely wrong. Years later, after I became a "new creation in Christ," I was healed of my learning disability; also my heavenly Father touched me and healed me from the negative words of my earthly father.

God's Word says it like this, "*There is one who speaks rashly like the thrust of a sword, but the tongue of the wise brings healing*" (Proverbs 12:18 AMP).

We are Responsible for Our Words

The Bible teaches us that our words have consequences.

I have to confess that this is a part of the Bible I wish were not written in there.

Matthew 12:36-37 says it plainly, "*But I say to you that for every idle word men may speak, they will give account of it on the Day of Judgment. For by your words you will be justified, and by your words you will be condemned.*" NKJV

To me, that is scarier than giants!

James says: "*So also the tongue is a small part of the body, and yet it boasts of great things. See how great a forest is set aflame by such a small fire! And the tongue is a fire, the very world of iniquity; the tongue is set among our members as that which defiles the entire body, and sets on fire the course of our life, and is set on fire by hell. For every species of beasts and birds, of reptiles and creatures of the sea, is tamed and has been tamed by the human race. But no one can tame the tongue; it is a restless evil and full of deadly poison. With it we bless our Lord and Father, and with it we curse men, who have been made in the likeness of God; from the same mouth come both blessing and cursing. My brethren, these things ought not to be this way*" (James 3:5-10 NASV).

WOW! The book of James says it very graphically, and tells it just like it is!

So what do we do with this?

Looking at verse ten, we find that both blessing and cursing can pour from the same mouth.

The greatest hypocrisy is that, with our words, we can bless and worship the God who created us, and five minutes later, curse someone who is made in the image of God.

The curses or negative words we receive from others, we can overcome. But how can we overcome the words we speak about ourselves?

You can overcome the negative words others say about you, but it's really hard to overcome the negative words you say about yourself!

Your question has to be, "How on earth can I overcome this? How can I ever do better with the words of my mouth?"

Well, the only way we can harness our tongue is by the continuous mercy and grace of God. It does us well to remember that "*His mercies begin afresh each morning*" (Lamentations 3:23 NLT).

The only way to learn to control your tongue is to

exercise *self*-control, which happens to be one of the fruits of the Spirit.

God's Word says it like this, "*But the fruit of the Spirit* [the result of His presence within us] *is love* [unselfish concern for others], *joy,* [inner] *peace, patience* [not the ability to wait, but how we act while waiting], *kindness, goodness, faithfulness, gentleness, self-control*" (Galatians 5:22-23 AMP).

When God listed the nine fruits of the Spirit, He put self-control last because the first eight fruits will not work without self-control.

Learn to Say What God Says

When the religious people confronted John the Baptist, they asked him, "*Then who are you? We need an answer for those who sent us. What do you have to say about yourself?*"

John replied in the words of the prophet Isaiah from 700 years earlier: "*I am a voice shouting in the wilderness, 'Clear the way for the Lord's coming!'*" (John 1:22-23 NET).

This is profound! When John answered the religious people, he answered by telling them who God said that he was!

All of us at one time or another go through difficult times, and, during these times, the last thing we need to do is listen to what the enemy says about us!

The very, very last thing we need to do is to listen

to a best friend's advice who is also confused, worried and depressed and has no clue of who he or she is in Christ!

The absolute best place to receive our self-worth and direction for our future is to listen to what God says about us.

Say with me now:

I am blessed!

I am a new creation!

I am a child of God!

I am made in God's image!

I am a masterpiece!

I am greatly loved!

God is love, and He loves me!

I am a friend of God!

We are God's creation and we were created to carry His Spirit. We have the potential to carry out His will. Our mission is to bring glory to His Name and reach a lost and dying world for Jesus.

Questions for Reflection:

1. **How have I injured others with the words of my mouth?**

2. **Am I willing to ask the Lord to help me to always speak words of blessings to others?**

Chip Fitz

I attend House on the Rock Church in Amite, La. About a week before the first service of the revival at Pastor Larry's church, I had an MRI of my head because of dizziness and sick spells. A few days before the revival, I received a call from the doctor's office stating that there was a spot on my brain and that they were scheduling another MRI for what type of treatment to pursue. My wife, Dee, and I attended the revival and were both baptized for healing and for more of God in our lives. The following Tuesday, the Neurologist called and wanted to meet with us before the follow-up MRI. He showed us a picture on his computer of the test and drew a yellow circle around a spot on the base of my brain and said that was a 6mm tumor, and showed us where it was blocking the nerves going into my inner ear. We did the follow-up MRI a week later and NO tumor! God is good all the time!

Chapter 12

Angels, Angels, Angels!

Are angels folklore? Are they found only in children's books? Are they figments of our imagination?

Or could it be that they are real?

In our recent revival meetings, one lady reported that she saw several angels in mid-air by the pool, where people were being baptized. Who knows what we could see if our eyes were always opened to the supernatural!

When I was really young, I remember seeing an old painting of two small children crossing a wooden bridge by themselves. The bridge was old and dangerous with a missing board. What I have never forgotten is that there was an enormous angel watching over the children as they crossed, and their faces showed no fear at all. I believe that the artist who painted that original image was inspired by the Holy Spirit.

Could it be that this picture represents the fact that there are angels watching over all of us, and that they are sometimes closer than we can imagine?

Once again, let's dig deep. I promise it will be worth it!

Angels are mentioned approximately 300 times in scripture.

God's Word says this:

Angels guard the tree of life in Heaven.

Angels announced the birth of Samson, John the Baptist, and Jesus.

An angel warned Joseph and Mary to escape to Egypt.

Angels were at the tomb of Jesus.

An angel appeared to Abraham and Hagar.

An angel appeared to Jacob in a dream.

The angel Gabriel appeared to Zechariah.

The angel Gabriel appeared to Mary, the mother of Jesus.

An angel appeared to Daniel in the lions' den.

An angel appeared to Cornelius in a dream.

An angel was with the apostle John on the Isle of Patmos when the book of Revelation was downloaded to him.

When we go through the scriptures, we can see clearly that angels are heavenly beings sent on assignments by God to intervene in the affairs of man.

Julienne Faucheux Hodges

I have battled severe depression my entire adult life. For several years, I was under a doctor's care and was prescribed a number of antidepressant medications, while also being counseled by a Christian therapist.

I knew in my heart that I had an unusual SPIRITUAL problem, not a chemical imbalance. No medication gave me relief.

In fact I had more intense depression from the medications. I tried to commit suicide four times. I've been off antidepressants since 2008, and have tried to fight it through prayer, ministry, nutrition, diet, and exercise, but have had only small victories.

In 2013, I entered a rehab for women to help me overcome this horrid

- continued next page -

Most people have not seen an angel, but there are those who have.

I've been asked why I have seen angels on a number of occasions. It might be because I have prayed off and on throughout my whole Christian life to see an angel. God really does care about the things that are important to us. If you start asking God to allow you to see into the spiritual realm, it just might happen!

Clarence the Angel

If you've seen the movie, "*It's a Wonderful Life*," you remember Clarence, the angel who rescued Jimmy Stewart from the river. That was all

Hollywood.

People do not become angels, and angels don't have to earn their wings.

So, what is the truth about angels?

Angels Were Created by God

Concerning angels, we find this in the Bible, "*For by Him all things were created in Heaven and on earth, [things] visible and invisible, whether thrones or dominions or rulers or authorities; all things were created and exist through Him [that is, by His activity] and for Him*" (Colossians 1:16 AMP).

Julienne continued

depression, returning after 22 months to continued daily struggle.

Many of my close friends at previous churches knew of my long struggles. My dear mother went through this enormous battle with me and did all that she could to help me through the years.

After years of my trying everything, THE LORD HAS FINALLY SET ME COMPLETELY FREE!

Upon attending the first Southeast Louisiana Revival service, at St. James Community Church in May, 2019, I went into the anointed baptismal waters and got completely healed of my lifelong battle with major depression.

I'm still so amazed at how I am truly healed and set free. It's been a year and I am still pinching myself because I have not been

- continued next page -

The scriptures tell us simply that all inanimate things in the universe, as well as earthly animals and man, were created in a span of six days.

However, scripture also tells us that when God laid the foundations of the earth, the angels shouted for joy. (Job 38:4-7 AMP)

There are pictures from the Renaissance that depict fat little baby angels with wings, but there is no scripture to support this. There are no baby maternity wards in Heaven, or nursing homes for the angels. Also, there are no scriptures to support that people become angels after they die. Have you ever been at a funeral and heard someone say of the deceased, "Well, I guess God needed another angel in Heaven"? When I hear that, I think, "You're deceived!"

Julienne Continued
attacked with depression. It feels so good to have the confidence of knowing I have the complete victory over it.
I am a walking miracle and I know the depths of pain that people who are vexed with depression are going through, because I lived with the dark cloud for so long, and thought it would never end. Today I am overjoyed because I know that the dark cloud of depression has no power over me. I'm living proof that God can and will set you free from your struggle.

God's Word does give us some insight into these incredible supernatural beings, so let's discover the truth about angels.

Fallen Angels

The scriptures teach that there was a war in Heaven, at which time a third of the angels were cast out of Heaven.

"*God did not even spare angels that sinned, but threw them into hell and sent them to pits of gloom to be kept there for judgment*" (2 Peter 2:4 AMP).

Like heavenly angels, but in an evil way, fallen angels can - and will, if they have the opportunity - intervene in the lives of men.

Heaven Will be Beyond our Wildest Imagination

The book of Isaiah gives us a priceless sneak preview into Heaven as its writer describes this scene:

"*Above Him seraphim* (heavenly beings) *stood; each one had six wings: with two wings he covered his face, with two wings he covered his feet, and with two wings he flew. And one called out to another, saying, 'Holy, Holy, Holy is the Lord of hosts; The whole earth is filled with His glory'*" (Isaiah 6:2-3).

WOW! What will it be like to be there? This is one awesome picture of heavenly beings that are beyond our comprehension!

We also learn that there are archangels: "*For the*

Lord Himself will come down from Heaven with a shout of command, with the voice of the archangel and with the [blast of the] *trumpet of God, and the dead in Christ will rise first"* (1Thessalonians 4:16 AMP).

So, as we read through the Bible, we get a glimpse into the existence of angels and their activities, even though they are obviously not the focus. Could it be that God lets us know just enough about angels that we will know they are there, that they have assignments, and that they are on the job?

There's Nothing New Under the Sun

If we keep a Biblical understanding of angels, we won't get off course and get wacky about them.

In fact, there's a warning for us in relation to our interaction with them:

> *"Don't let anyone declare you lost when you refuse to worship angels, as they say you must"* (Colossians 2:18 TLB).

This scripture was written in the first century; at that time people were worshiping statues, angels, Jesus' mother, and praying to dead people. As the Bible tells us, there's nothing new under the sun. Angels are not to be worshiped! Any message that is given by an angel should always line up with God's Word.

Listen to the warnings God gives us. He makes it

clear:

> "*And no wonder, since Satan himself masquerades himself as an angel of light*" (2 Corinthians 11:14 AMP).

> "*But even if we, or an angel from Heaven, should preach to you a gospel contrary to that which we [originally] preached to you, let him be condemned to destruction!*"(Galatians 1:8 AMP)

When You Feel Surrounded, Angels Are Near

So far, we've seen that angels are supernatural beings who have a message to deliver. They are on assignment to believers and unbelievers.

> "*Are they not ministering spirits sent forth to minister for those who will inherit salvation?*" (Hebrews 1:14 NKJV)

The Word confirms that He "*...makes His angels spirits and His ministers a flame of fire*" (Hebrews 1:7 NKJV).

One of my favorite stories of angels is the story of Elisha and his servant, who were surrounded by the Syrian army. Elisha's servant was fearful and was sure that they were about to die, but the servant couldn't see what Elisha could see. It is recorded that he comforted his servant in this manner:

> "*Do not fear, for those who are with us are more than those who are with them.*"

Elisha prayed, saying, "*Lord, I pray, open his eyes that he may see. Then the Lord opened the eyes of the young man, and he saw. And behold, the mountain was full of horses and chariots of fire all around Elisha*" (2 Kings 6:16-17 NKJV).

If we were able to see into the realm of the supernatural, just imagine what things we would be able to see!

The apostle Paul left us with this wisdom: "*So we look not at the things which are seen, but at the things which are unseen; for the things which are visible are temporal [just brief and fleeting], but the things which are invisible are everlasting and imperishable*" (2 Corinthians 4:18 AMP).

When You Are Outnumbered, Angels Are There

One of the great benefits of being able to read God's Word is that we can see how men and women of faith overcame insurmountable odds.

The story of Gideon is so encouraging to us all. Gideon started off to war with 32,000 men, facing three enemy kings. The Bible describes the size of their forces this way:

> "*Now the Midianites and the Amalekites and all the sons of the east were lying [camped] in the valley, as countless as locusts; and their camels were without number, as numerous as the sand on the seashore*" (Judges 7:12 AMP).

God told Gideon to do something that makes no sense in the natural realm. He had Gideon reduce his forces down to 300 men. When Gideon followed God's instructions, the enemy ended up turning their swords against each other in the darkness of night. If Gideon would not have obeyed the Lord, and fought the battle with his original 32,000 men, he would have died that day.

This story speaks loud and clear to us who love the Lord! When we obey what the Lord tells us, we enter a supernatural realm where God fights our battles for us! I learned a long time ago, if I try to defend myself, that's all the defense I get. If I allow God to defend me, He does a great job.

When we think about epic battles recorded in scripture, God's people were always outnumbered!

Angels Are Sent to Minister to Us

Ok, hold on, because this is where it gets really good!

Almost anyone, even people who do not believe in God, would agree that there are unseen evil forces that will whisper to our soul (our mind, will, and emotions). They tempt us with thoughts like this: "You deserve better. You aren't appreciated. You need a more expensive one; just charge it. No one will know. You aren't loved. Get a divorce; that will solve everything!"

Come on now, tell me, if a demon from hell can interject a temptation to lie, steal, commit adultery, look at pornography, or gossip, couldn't an angel on assignment be sitting right next to you ministering God's Word to your spirit?

You bet your sweet blessing he can!

In fact, scripture gives us reason to believe they throw a party of sorts! Something special happens each time someone gives his life to the Lord! If you find that hard to believe, check this out:

> *"Well, in the same way Heaven will be happier over one lost sinner who returns to God than over ninety-nine others who haven't strayed away!... In the same way there is joy in the presence of the angels of God when one sinner repents"* (Luke 15:7&10 NLT).

Angel Sightings

Years ago, my father-in-law, who was a very godly man, was in the hospital near the end of his life. On my last visit with him, as I stood by his bed in the hospital room, he pointed to the wall and said, "Those are the most beautiful flowers I've ever seen. There are no flowers on earth that look that beautiful!"

Then he motioned toward the doorway in his room and asked, "Who are those men in white clothes?"

When I turned to look there was no one there, just a closed door. About a week later he went home to be with the Lord.

Another time, my wife, Rinalda, was running some errands in Baton Rouge, Louisiana, with our girls, who were ten and eleven years old. Her car died right in the middle of a busy intersection. As soon as it happened, a stranger appeared at the side of the car and said, "Ma'am, do you need help?"

She said yes, and before she knew what happened, he had pushed the car by hand, by himself, to safety. As Rinalda got out of the car to thank him, he had disappeared. My girls were shocked that he was nowhere in sight.

God's Word reminds us in this next passage that we should always be kind to everyone, because angels can sometimes appear to us as ordinary people:

> "*Let love of your fellow believers continue. Do not neglect to extend hospitality to strangers* [especially among the family of believers - being friendly, cordial, and gracious, sharing the comforts of your home and doing your part generously], *for by this some have entertained angels without knowing it*" (Hebrews 13:1-2 AMP).

Years ago, while we were missionaries in Russia, we had been unable to have children, and we were working on an adoption. We had spent a great deal of time trying to adopt, and our hearts' desire was to have exactly the baby that God wanted us to have.

One day I got a phone call from a Russian lady,

asking if I was the American she heard about who was looking for a baby girl. I speak very broken Russian, but by some miracle, I was able to make arrangements for us to meet her in a city four hours away.

The next day, my wife and I left Moscow in our little Russian car in the predawn hours, with two feet of snow on the ground. As I looked out of my windshield, there was an angel at least ten feet tall with his arm outstretched. He was positioned just off my right fender, pointing in the direction we were headed. He was translucent and almost looked like an ice sculpture.

I said, "Oh, oh, look, oh," pointing to the right front fender of the car. My wife asked what was there. She couldn't see him. Only I saw him, but at that moment I knew that the meeting would result in our adoption being successful.

We also have a daughter that was born by promise. My wife, Rinalda, kept telling me that God had given her a word that she would have a baby before she turned forty.

As the years ticked by and we had no children I began to wonder if she had really heard from Heaven. Our oldest daughter was supposed to be in our home by the end of May, but she didn't arrive until September.

But around the first week of May, we were out in Moscow, and Rinalda stopped for moment. She said she had the strangest feeling, as though something miraculous had just happened.

By June, she knew she was pregnant, but I wasn't sure. I made her take three home pregnancy tests to confirm it.

Victoria made her debut on February 1, 1999. Rinalda was thirty-nine years and 311 days old. She had heard from Heaven; we had not one, but two babies before she turned forty years old!

Now that's God!

You Have Personal Angels Assigned to You

The Jewish people believed that each person has a personal angel, and possibly, more than one. We can see this in the following Biblical discourses.

Peter's friends were praying for his release from prison when something miraculous occurred. This is how it's recorded:

> "*Recognizing Peter's voice, in her joy she failed to open the gate, but ran in and announced that Peter was standing in front of the gateway. They said to her, 'You are out of your mind!' But she kept insisting that it was so. They kept saying, 'It is his angel!'*" (Acts 12:14-15 ESV).

Then we read what Jesus said in Matthew's gospel: "*See that you do not despise or think less of one of these little ones, for I say to you that their angels in Heaven* [are in the presence of and] *continually look upon the face of My Father who is in Heaven*" (Matthew 18:10 AMP).

Just imagine, we are so valuable to God that we have been assigned personal angels. The big question is this: If you have personal angels assigned to you, what do they hear you say? If you remember, Proverbs 18 says that "*Life and death are in the power of the tongue.*"

And then there's Psalm 103:20, "*Bless the Lord, you His angels, You mighty ones who do His commandments, obeying the voice of His Word!*" (AMP).

Our job as believers is to obey God's Word, speak His Word, seek His will, carry out His will, and live in God's plan for our lives. What your angels need to be saying is, "WOW, this guy (or this girl) has got it going on! What a great assignment this is; we are gonna have some great adventures together!"

The last thing you want your angels saying is, "What a stinking assignment; all this character does is whine and complain about every single thing in life!"

Are angels involved in revival? Absolutely!

In chapter one, I told the story of a great move of the Spirit that took place in our men's prayer meeting, of men being blown back as they approached the microphone, one man having a hand laid on his shoulder, but with no one there.

This was all angelic activity, and the beginning of our revival.

We need to look at it like this - if angels are assigned to believers, and revivals are a place where believers gather together with an unusually high level of expectation, I would say that revivals are a place where our angels definitely love to hang out.

Questions for Reflection:

1. **Is it possible that angels have been assigned to my life?**

2. **Do I remember a time where an angel may have ministered to me or directed my life?**

Chapter 13

The "If Only" of Human Reason

With some 7.8 billion people alive on the earth today, we could only imagine how many of them said this very day, "God, if only I knew you were there!"

A friend of mine mentioned to someone about all the wonderful things that God is presently doing in our revival, and the person's response was, "If only I could believe that God does those things today!"

God is there! He is a great God who desperately loves His children, and often intervenes in the lives of man.

For that recently divorced single mom that is saying, "God, if only I knew you were there!"

For that person struggling in a new business, saying, "God, if only I knew which way to turn!"

What about that person who was hurt by a church leader, or the church leader that was hurt by church members, saying, "God, if you only knew my pain!"

There are some who have lost everything. You might even be saying, "God, if only you could put my life back together!"

If you are a person without a clue in the world what to do with the rest of your life, I'm sure you've thought, "If only God could give me direction!"

If you happen to be the pastor of a church, you may have been asking, "God, where are you? If only you would show me what to do!"

For you – whoever you are and however you might be struggling – the answer is not a new curriculum, not a fresh marketing plan, not a new spouse, or a hot new sermon series.

Your answer is to diligently seek God!

I can tell you from personal experience that God is there. He does know your pain. He really does care, and He knows how to put things back together.

The "If Only" of Broken-heartedness

Everywhere we look, there are hurting people.

Many are hurt through broken relationships, others through personal failure, the loss of a loved one – the list goes on. People try everything, from counseling to medicating the problem. With human reason, we might conclude that this is just life! This is just the way it is, and you just have to live with it. Your situation is impossible!

God, in His Word, acknowledges your situation,

your broken-heartedness, and He says that your situation is NOT impossible.

After the rich young ruler walked away downcast, in the face of what seemed impossible, Jesus looked at His disciples and assured them, *"With men this is impossible, but all things are possible with God"* (Matthew 19:26 AMP).

Broken-hearted people say, "If only God could heal me!"

But the Word of God says that He heals the brokenhearted!

Psalm 147:3 tells us, *"He heals the brokenhearted and binds up their wounds."* The Amplified Bible adds, *"curing their pains and their sorrows."*

The "If Only" of Divorce

Religion has done a great job of making divorced people feel like second-class citizens.

On top of that, they believe they are damaged goods, and who would ever love them?

The divorce rate in America is about fifty percent right now. Experts say it is dropping slightly, but it appears the reason for the slight drop is because fewer people are getting married nowadays. They just live together!

Human reasoning tells people that marriage doesn't work, so they decide, "I don't want to get divorced again, so I'll just shack up!"

Whether you call it "shacking up" or "living in sin," God calls it fornication.

Well, we just saw how human reason can get us out of the frying pan and into the fire. The answer to a failed relationship is not a new romance. When your marriage ends in shambles, before you try another marriage, it's best to find out what God's guidelines for marriage are.

The last thing you should want to do is to bring the same old you into a new relationship.

When people decide to follow God's guidelines the next time around, it's truly amazing to see what God can do in their lives! Never ever say, "If only I could love again," or "If only someone could love me!"

There is a God in Heaven that makes all things new. All things are possible to him who believes!

"If Only" I Could Find a Great Church

Someone once said, "Not everyone in church is a Christian."

It seems that so many people today really do want God in their lives, but because there are people in churches who don't have Christian qualities, they will have nothing to do with church. They have been hurt by a church member or leader. And while, deep down, they want to go to church, they just can't find the right one.

I hear people say, "I'm just so happy sitting home,

worshiping God by myself."

Others have started little groups whose purpose is to fellowship and grow in the Lord, but reject being labeled a church.

Each of these scenarios was birthed in offense; someone hurt them and they blamed the church.

What church-hurt people fail to realize is that, regardless of what organization or group anyone seeks to be part of, the danger of being hurt or offended exists there.

People can get hurt in any type of relationship. We get hurt at work, but do we quit work? Hopefully not.

The plain truth is that the enemy likes nothing better than to see a child of God – one filled with untold potential and giftings – sidelined because of hurt or offense.

Some say, "The people in church should know better."

Of course they should know better! Both those who hurt and those who get offended at being hurt should know better. However, is it right to judge the whole church for the wrong actions of a few? Of course not!

People sometimes use Ephesians 5:27 to find fault with the church. It says that Jesus is coming back for a bride without spot or wrinkle. They take that scripture to mean that Jesus cannot return again until everyone in every church "gets their act together." If that were the case, He would never return!

I see in scripture that believers are hidden in Christ; at the moment of salvation, you are washed clean of your sins, and from that point on, when God looks at you, He no longer sees your sin.

The book of Colossians reveals that our old life is dead and our new life is hidden in Christ:

"For you died [to this world], and your [new, real] life is hidden with Christ in God. When Christ, who is our life, appears, then you also will appear with Him in glory" (Colossians 3:3-4 AMP).

Under Construction

I like to say it like this: everyone in our church is a mess, and so am I. We are all a work in progress. It would be great if we all wore ball caps that said, "Under Construction. God's not finished with me yet!"

We all have flesh to deal with. Human reason is what makes us judge people. It's especially bad when we judge the Church, the body of Christ that Jesus has judged as having been washed in His blood.

The book of 2 Corinthians calls us the righteousness of God in Christ Jesus:

"For He made Him who knew no sin to be sin for us, that we might become the righteousness of

God in Him" (2 Corinthians 5:21 NKJV).

God's Word says this:

> "*For with what judgment you judge, you will be judged; and with the measure you use, it will be measured back to you*" (Matthew 7:2 NKJV).

That's scary!

I believe that the scripture points out that the Church is not perfect, but it is filled with people who are called out of the world and called into a relationship with God.

When we are hurt or disappointed by another Christian, instead of blaming the Church as a whole, we should forgive. After all, scripture tells us over and over to forgive.

> "*Be kind and compassionate to one another, forgiving each other, just as in Christ God forgave you*" (Ephesians 4:32 NIV).

In fact, God's Word tells us that, if we do not forgive, we cannot be forgiven. (See Mark 11:25-26)

In the second chapter of Acts, we see the birth of the early Church. The remainder of the New Testament is comprised of epistles written to the various churches about everything from how the churches were started to how to live as believers.

When we stop and think how Jesus referred to the Church, He made it very personal. If you listen closely, you can hear Jesus' love for the Church when He referred to it as "My Church." Read what He said:

"Upon this rock I will build My church, and all the powers of hell will not conquer it" (Matthew 16:18 NLT).

Hell will not conquer His Church! Just imagine for a moment all the people who are sitting at home alone and isolated, not involved in a local church - despite the fact that they love the Lord!

They could be using their giftings, talents, and resources, going on adventurous mission trips or funding world missions. Think of the sweet fellowship they could be having with other believers and the hurting people they could be touching with the love of God.

If only we could see that human reason keeps us divided!

The Word of God says in John 17:21 (NJKV) that Jesus desires us to be as one. When we make a decision to make things right with those who have wronged us, no matter what the cost, we will be amazed to see the restoration that God can bring.

My advice is to go back to the church that you were hurt in, forgive them, and ask forgiveness for anything you might have done. I promise you, you will see the wonder-working power of God go before you in His grace and mercy.

One of the biggest steps we can take toward

reviving the Church is the revival and restoration of our own hearts to the love shed abroad in them by our Father.

When God restores a heart He makes it better than it was before.

Questions for Reflection:

1. What are the "If Only's" of my life that hinder me?

2. Ask the Lord to help you overcome them.

Nick.

I was born and raised Southern Baptist. I always prayed daily and I thought all was well. When I heard about the baptism of fire and water, I wasn't skeptical, but stand-offish. I was diagnosed with a bad kidney that had to be removed immediately! I went to the baptism in Paulina, Louisiana, February 7, 2020, with my family. I asked for spiritual cleansing and physical healing. As soon as I stepped into the pool I felt God's presence. My whole body began to tremble uncontrollably. When I received prayer, I was slain by the Spirit for the first time in my life! My life has totally changed! He chose not to remove the cancer that was in my kidney, but allowed the kidney to be removed with the cancer contained in it! Praise God! This experience has caused me to seek Him in a whole new way. And I would highly recommend to anyone who is considering it: just go for it!

Chapter 14

Getting Rid of Your "If Only" Once and For All

There are literally thousands of books, articles, and even dot.coms, advising people how to find God.

First of all, God is not lost, and He hasn't forgotten about us. The Bible tells the story of the prodigal son, relating that he had been lost, but now was found. We are all born as sinners in need of a Savior.

When we are presented with the Gospel at some time in our lives, we have the opportunity to receive salvation. After salvation, if we get caught up in the business of life, juggling family and work, we might fail in our efforts to make time for God, and many become nominal Christians, attending church once a month maybe, but never really fulfilling their God given destiny.

Once you receive salvation, your life is now supernatural. But you still live in a natural world. We read this in God's supernatural Word: *"Beloved, I urge you as aliens and strangers [in this world] to abstain from the sensual urges* [those dishonorable desires] *that wage war against the soul*" (1 Peter 2:11 AMP).

Over the years, I have seen person after person, family after family, who have had tremendous calls of God on their lives. Some who were called to be pastors are now working different jobs, their families are in disaster and they often wonder, *What if I had answered the call!*

Some were called to be worship leaders and are now singing in barrooms. Some, called to be church elders, are now chasing the American dream. Others were called to be missionaries, but are now working two jobs to make ends meet.

The pressures of the world are many. The world has more than enough options: if it can't get you tied up with the NFL or the NBA, it will get you tied up in Little League sports. Chasing things that, well, even if you caught them, they couldn't give you what you are looking for.

As a pastor, I have the unique opportunity of hearing people's regrets toward the end of their lives. One thing that I always hear is, "I wish I would have been able to do more for the Lord." The real question that so many are asking themselves is, "How do I get myself out of this mess?"

Some people assume that God is being purposely elusive or trying to play a game of hide and seek. That is not the case at all. God's Word cautions us about presuming with our limited understanding:

"For as the heavens are higher than the earth, so are My ways higher than your ways, and My thoughts than your thoughts" (Isaiah 55:9).

If you have read this far, it's because you are desperate for God, so what I'm about to tell you will help you with "if only" thoughts. This is not something I learned from a book; nor is it a theory. This is from my own experience. There are well over 7,000 promises in God's Word, and many are promises that He will answer us.

Here is one of my favorite promises; I call it, God's telephone number – 5015:

> *"Call on Me in the day of trouble; I will rescue you, and you shall honor and glorify Me"* (Psalm 50:15 AMP).

The Supernatural Realm of Worship and Prayer

Worship and prayer are not natural, but they are the spiritual tool that results in a relationship with God, the Creator of all things!

Hebrews 11:6 says, *"But without faith it is impossible to* [walk with God and] *please Him, for whoever comes* [near] *to God must* [necessarily] *believe that God exists and that He rewards those who* [earnestly and diligently] *seek Him"* (AMP).

Many people seek God, but how many really seek him diligently? Maybe, our answer is right in front of us!

The New Testament was written in the Greek language, and the Greek word for "diligently seeking" can also be translated as "seek out," "seek out after," "require," "investigate," "crave," "demand," "worship."

Wow! Is this amazing!

Worship is part of diligently seeking after God.

What I'm talking about is not singing some songs at church on Sunday morning. I'm talking about getting alone and worshiping daily with the determination that, "I'm gonna do this, and I'm gonna do it just because I love the Lord, and I'm so thankful for all He's already done for me!"

This is the heart of worship.

If King David lived in today's world, he might be like every Christian who has a couple dozen books on how to live the successful Christian life. However, David did not receive his anointing from the latest book or sermon series; I believe he got it from spending time with the Lord!

Just before David became the king of Israel, his anointing as a worshiper would soothe King Saul who was tormented by evil spirits. I believe that young David received his powerful anointing as a shepherd boy worshiping the Lord alone in the fields under star-filled nights.

You might say, "I can't play an instrument." That's quite alright; you don't need to. Today, everyone has a phone that can deliver some of the world's best worship music directly to you.

We Spend Our Time on What We Value

Think of it like this: worship involves us setting aside the time to "focus on, spending time with and meditating on what we adore." We all have the same amount of time each day; no one gets a minute more.

We know what we value by what we spend time doing.

What we focus on and spend time doing is what we apprehend and what apprehends us. What would happen if some of us made a firm decision to get our face in His Book and not in FaceBook! Just a reminder: all those people on FaceBook are really not your friends!

If you want to apprehend God, you will have to diligently seek Him. This is possible, and you can do it! What I'm talking about is doable. If it were not possible, God would never have suggested for us to seek diligently after Him.

It's Not About a Formula; It's About Desperation

What I'm about to tell you can't be taught: it has to be caught. What I mean is that you have to receive this by revelation knowledge. When a person receives salvation, his or her spirit becomes alive in Christ. That person may still live in that old body, but there must be a hunger for God's Word, a desire to see others come to Christ, a desire to be in the house of the Lord, and a desire for fellowship.

The key is to seek God's face, not His gifts. When we seek His face, the gifts follow.

We have become "new creations." God's Word says it like this, "*Therefore, if anyone is in Christ, he is a new creation; old things have passed away; behold, all things have become new*" (2 Corinthians 5:17 NKJV).

Here's the problem: even though we are a totally new creation, we still live in a fallen world with the constant pressures of a job, children, parents and, many times, the constant pressures of unsaved relatives.

We have our church family who encourages us to be all that God wants us to be. But then our old friends say something like, "I remember when you used to be fun to be around." Take some good advice: those "old friends" are exactly the people you do not need to be around.

If you want what someone else has, you'll have to do what they did to get it!

When we see people owning things that we could only wish we owned, chances are that they worked hard to get them. The same is true about people who seem to be much more spiritual than we are; believe me, they didn't just wake up with an amazing relationship with God.

It's like I always say about marriage: your marriage is like a garden, and what you plant in your marriage will grow. What you put into your relationship with God, you will get out. If you put in the time, you will get results.

God isn't hiding from you; He wants you to seek Him!

Likewise, diamonds, rubies and precious metals are not found on the surface of the ground, you have to dig for them.

At one time or another, we are all desperate to hear from God. We may need direction for our marriage, ministry, business, or career. When we spend time in personal worship and prayer, these are the things that move the heart of God.

You've Read Everything Just to Read This

When you say, "If Only God," in relation to your current situation, you just said what you really believe: that you really doubt God's ability to work in your life!

People say:

If only I knew God was real. (He is.)

If only God knew my situation. (He does.)

If only I knew God could hear me. (He can.)

If only I knew He would answer. (He will.)

Make an appointment with God; He's waiting for you!

The End Times and End-Time Revivals

As I am writing the last pages of this book, we are in the midst of the Covid-19 pandemic. Many are preaching doom and gloom. More than ever before, people believe we are in the very beginnings of the end times; however, I believe that we are about to see the beginning of the great end-time revivals. How do I back this up scripturally?

Jesus said it like this, *"Nation will go to war against nation, and kingdom against kingdom, there will be great earthquakes, and there will be famines and plagues in many lands"* (Luke 21:10 NLT)

These things are happening right now!

In the Old Testament, the prophet Joel said there would be a great end-time revival or "outpouring" of God's Spirit: *"It shall come about after this, that I shall pour out My Spirit on all mankind"* (Joel 2:28 AMP).

Some believe that this coming revival will happen in the end times; others think it will happen during the millennium, when Christ returns. I believe they are both correct.

Could it be possible that this great outpouring mentioned in the book of Joel is happening in a larger time period?

We have to remember that, with the Lord, *"one*

day is as a thousand years, and a thousand years as one day," according to 2 Peter 3:8. (NKJV)

I believe that this great outpouring has been happening periodically since the time of the book of Acts, because, when Peter preached on the day of Pentecost, he cited Joel 2:28 to explain what was happening on that very day!

Yes, look at it for yourself: "*And it shall come to pass in the last days, says God, that I will pour out of My Spirit on all flesh*" (Acts 2:17-18 NKJV).

There it is! So all of the "revivals" - or should we say outpourings - of God's Spirit, from the book of Acts until what we see happening today, are end-time revivals.

With all that in mind, Jesus said in Matthew that one of the signs of the end times will be offenses. Jesus said it like this, "*And then many will be offended, will betray one another, and will hate one another*" (Matthew 24:10).

This is absolutely true! However, what we are seeing happen in our revivals is something truly supernatural. We have witnessed, first-hand, people rising above their petty offenses, and, more than ever before, we will see people putting God first in their lives!

I believe we are on the edge of the great end-time revival, the likes of which we have never seen. I believe that we are about to see great moves of His Holy Spirit and demonstrations of God's great love!

Isn't God good!

Too long have we lived in the land of "If Only"!

It is no longer about "If Only, God..."

What God started in our men's meetings is about to begin more and more.

What God began in the North Georgia Revival in Dawsonville and the Southeast Louisiana Revival is beginning to spill over everywhere that people are willing to diligently seek Him.

Revival always began with one or two.

Revival in Wales began with Evan Roberts.

Revival in the Hebrides began with the Smith sisters.

Revival on Azusa Street began with William Seymore.

Revival today begins with YOU!

Revival in your family begins with you!

Revival in your church begins with you!

Revival in your city begins with you!

This is what revival is all about.

Revival is a result of men praying and God responding.

Revival is a supernatural WAKE-UP CALL!

Revival is re-establishing your commitment to God!

Revival is repenting for compromising your values!

Revival is a return to holiness!

When people pray, God responds with a divine appointment.

Whole churches need revival! People need revival in their individual lives! Families don't need new family rules; they need revival! Cities need revival!

If I could define revival, I would say that revival is the Holy Spirit responding to the desperate and unrelenting prayers of a people who have humbled themselves before God.

More than anything, revival is an opportunity to hit the RESET BUTTON, so the Holy Spirit can redirect your life!

Revival is an invitation from the Lord to humble ourselves and get back on track with Him. No matter how off-course we've gotten, God is saying to each and every one of us, "Come with Me. Let's finish well!"

Chapter 15

And Now, a Few Words from the Pastors of the Southeastern Louisiana Revival...

Because this revival has been momentous for the body of Christ in Louisiana and the entire Deep South region – and because we believe it will become even more momentous as the Holy Spirit continues it – we would like to share with you the impressions from some of the ministers who have been leaders in this work of God.

Pastor Testimonies:

Pastor Rinalda Rocquin, "Bury Me In Russia"

In the summer of 1992, Larry and I went on a crusade to Ivanovo, Russia, to help plant a new church. It was a life-changing trip. We had graduated from Bible school the year before, and had been praying for God to show us His will for our lives.

While we were there, God spoke loud and clear that Russia was our new assignment.

After arriving home, we started the process of becoming full-time missionaries. Life was exciting! In one meeting, we were asked a question that rather startled us: If we were to die in Russia, where would we want to be buried, in America or Russia?

After much prayer and discussion, Larry and I decided, if God had called us to Russia and we were to die there, then bury us in Russia. So the motto, "Bury me in Russia," was born. We were one hundred percent committed to our call to Russia, willing to stay until we died.

After eight years in Russia, God called us back to America to pastor in Paulina, Louisiana. So our motto was changed to, "Bury me in Paulina." We were excited to pastor the church in Paulina! We knew God had spoken to both of us, and we were totally committed to our new assignment.

We came to a church that had been through a difficult time and many people were hurt. Those first years were both hard and rewarding. And then the years just seemed to march on. We saw God moving, but on a very small scale.

We wanted more! We had to have more! We wanted revival.

For me, adjusting back to American life took longer than I expected. I missed our team in Russia, plus the constant contact with other missionaries and pastors. I felt like I had been dropped off in a sugar cane field and forgotten. I enjoyed raising my girls in a small town and I loved our church family, but I missed the relationships with other ministers.

Sometimes I really felt alone, but I knew God had called us here and we would see Him do amazing things if we just stayed planted where He had placed us.

Life can change so suddenly. For us, it was one trip to North Georgia and one healed back. With that, two lives were changed forever. We could not believe what had happened. God healed Larry's back and then He said, "Share it. Don't just be happy that you are healed."

You read the story, so you know how the Southeast Louisiana Revival was born. Now every month, five churches come together and host the revival. I find myself in the midst of friends and ministers, and relationships have been birthed and strengthened. Churches are working together with one common goal: REVIVAL.

Revival has changed us, personally, as well as our church. We have always had a sweet, loving church, but through the revival I saw people growing and changing right before my eyes.

I saw people set free from addictions, healed physically, emotionally and mentally, and relationships restored. I saw a church family start working together in unity like never before, a team of believers doing whatever it took to host the revival, without complaining about it. People were willing to come early and stay late - I mean, real late: two, three o'clock in the morning - and then come back on Saturday morning to clean up and get ready for Sunday.

I saw two members of our church who had been at odds for years totally restored. One even told me, "...like it never happened."

REVIVAL has come! And this is just the beginning!

Pastor Rinalda Rocquin, St. James Community Church

Pastor Sonny Wahl

The Southeast Louisiana Revival came at a time when our church was experiencing tremendous moves of God and sweet times of visitation.

I've been in the ministry for thirty years and have seen the good, the bad, and the ugly in church meetings and revivals! In my pride I thought, 'We've already got revival in our meetings, so we will just stay in our building and you in yours.'

When Pastor Larry reported to me that he had just been healed of a serious debilitating back condition at the Georgia Revival, the Lord spoke to my heart, 'Attend, serve and unify the body.'

Well, when God speaks, it's best to listen, and do it His Way!

At first, I was very hesitant to engage and participate in the meetings. But everything changed when I saw the hunger and expectancy of the people entering the baptismal pool. People were truly getting touched, healed and changed by God! Children, young teens, elderly, hipsters, cutters, couples, and people of every type came wading into the water to meet God.

I witnessed so many receiving deliverance, healing, Holy Spirit baptism, shaking, breakthroughs with tears and rejoicing. Young children were coming out of the water sharing open visions of angels and the Lord Jesus! Entire families baptized simultaneously, emerging from the waters holding onto one another in sweet reunion. Veteran ministers who were badly hurt, damaged, and burned out from years of ministry, were being healed, refreshed and their callings of God revived and restored!

This was more than a new-believers water baptism experience; this was a true encounter with God! There was fire on the water and the Holy Spirit was everywhere.

As I prayed and loved on these wonderful people of faith, layers of religion and hardness began melting away, leaving my heart tender and more open to trust and love again. God even used these meetings to heal and restore a damaged relationship between Pastor Larry and myself, from a messy church transition many years ago.

Now both churches are free to flow and grow with God because the leadership is flowing in unity, forgiveness and in Christ's love.

The greatest fruit of the Southeast Louisiana Outpouring has been the new friendships with the pastors and their wives, with whom I have had the honor to work over the past several months. They all have been so giving and loving, with no agendas or ambitions. What a great and refreshing season!

Great things are ahead for the Southeast Louisiana Revival, and I believe God will continue to build His Kingdom in this atmosphere of love, humility, prayer, and unity.

Pastor Sonny Wahl, Senior Pastor Praise Church, Prairieville, LA

Pastors Jeff and Tammy McKneely

We will never be the same.

We have been pastors for sixteen years and have never wanted church to be just church. I think all of us enter ministry as passionate pursuers of God, leading us to love and ultimately shepherd people. But without even realizing it, we begin to minister more and more to people and less and less to God.

We were so excited when Larry told us about how God was moving in the North Georgia Revival and invited us to participate here in Louisiana. I would be lying if I didn't say that my first thought was, 'This could be great for our people.' But I was the one needing a fresh touch from God.

Tammy and I looked forward to the Southeast Louisiana Revival (SLR) at St. James in April with great anticipation of God moving.

The first night, as Pastor Todd Smith shared his heart, I heard the Kingdom of God preached and my heart burned. After Todd's message each night, Jesus moved mightily in the waters of baptism, with signs and wonders and healing and deliverance and baptism of the Holy Spirit and freedom and abundant life and Kingdom!!!

After baptizing hundreds of people in that cold swimming pool until after midnight, it was our opportunity to be baptized. Jesus wrecked us in the water. He touched us and changed us.

Our lives and our church haven't been the same since.

We have a focused pursuit to host His presence. Our building is open for 24/7 prayer, with worship music streaming in the sanctuary.

Leading up to our hosting the SLR at House on the Rock in June, we began earnestly seeking the presence of God with prayer, fasting, teaching, worship, resting, and waiting. We became desperate for His presence.

People come daily just to minister to the Lord, asking nothing from Him. God has used the SLR to transform us. We are growing in the Spirit of God and now have a greater capacity to love God and to love people.

Yes, we have seen supernatural healing miracles. We have seen backs, knees, shoulders, addictions, emotions, and tumors instantly healed. But the greatest miracle that we have seen is Jesus touching us in the water. We have seen Jesus do more in one night of baptisms than in years of discipleship classes, counseling, or Bible studies. We have seen the altar filled with people after midnight! On a school night!! When there wasn't even an altar call!!!

We also cherish the special unity of believers with the pastors and churches. By unity, I don't mean that we tolerate each other in order to work together for the greater good. I mean that we love each other and look forward to spending time with each other. We celebrate and encourage each other. We are focused on hosting His Presence and fulfilling Jesus' prayer: 'Your Kingdom come. Your will be done on Earth as it is in Heaven.'

As we write this, we have been unable to hold in-person services for the last seven weeks due to the Covid-19 restrictions in Louisiana. God is so faithful and gracious to us. Through the NGR and the SLR, he prepared us all to host His presence, not just in the church building, but in our homes.

Pastors Jeff and Tammy McKneely, House on the Rock Church, Amite, LA

Pastor Mervin Strother

When true revival touches people and a region, genuine change occurs. I have been blessed to be a part of the Southeast Louisiana Revival for the past year and a half. I am so grateful to Pastor Larry and Rinalda Rocquin for having a heart to pursue revival and bring other pastors along on the journey.

I have seen lives touched from our church, our region and even around the world. The first three nights of the Southeast Louisiana Revival in Paulina, LA, were impactful and life changing. As we gathered, I was not sure what to expect. Was God going to move? Was he going to touch people as He had been doing in Dawsonville, at the North Georgia Revival?

Let me tell you, God showed up in a powerful way! Hearts were changed, people repented, and people were filled with the Holy Spirit. No show, no pumping people up, no hype, no glamour – just the presence of God gently (and sometimes powerfully) encountering His people as they stepped into the waters of baptism.

As a by-product of people repenting and turning their hearts to the Lord, many physical healings manifested.

I have been in the pastoral ministry for the past twenty-seven years. I have counseled scores of people and observed church members being counseled for years. We love the ministry of counseling and understand its purpose and place in the body of Christ. After all, counseling is simply trying to get people with needs to understand and apply the Word of God to their lives.

One thing I have observed with the Southeast Louisiana Revival is that some of the people who have been counseled for years, with minimal results, were touched and set free by entering the baptismal waters of revival. Praise the Lord!

Shortly after our first revival in Paulina, I set out on a ten-day Journey to Brazil with a fellow pastor and former missionary. If God was touching people through baptism in Georgia, and now in Louisiana, would He touch people in Brazil, also?

The answer is yes!

As we brought the Southeast Louisiana Revival to four Brazilian cities, we saw around one thousand people baptized with incredible fruit. I have never witnessed so many people baptized in the Holy Spirit in such a short period of time as I did on this trip.

As we have continued with the Southeast Louisiana Revival in different locations, the results have been the same: God coming with peace, His presence, anointing, fire, deliverance, healing and reconciliation, as Jesus meets His people in the water.

Let God Arise! Let His enemies be scattered!

Pastor Mervin Strother, Cornerstone Church, Amite, LA

Pastor Donnie Shaffer

I became part of the Southeast Louisiana Revival through two means: 1. My friendship with Pastor Larry Rocquin. (We attended MTI Bible College together, graduating in 1991. Larry went to Russia and I went to Brazil. Then after more than a decade on the mission field, we both found ourselves pastoring local churches in Southeast Louisiana.) 2. Then there was the testimony of healing that Larry had for his back pain.

I will admit I had a certain hesitancy when Larry first told me of his experience at Christ Fellowship Church in Dawsonville, GA. He was on fire about this revival where people were being baptized in water, even if they had already been baptized.

And people were being healed!

Larry's suggestion was that we join our churches together and invite Pastor Todd Smith to hold one of these baptisms here in Southeast Louisiana.

Well, that first meeting we held at Larry's church ended up involving five local pastors and their churches. I was very impressed with Pastor Todd and the unity I saw as these five pastors worked together with a common goal: REVIVAL.

The quality that stood out most was a deep and genuine repentance on the part of those being baptized. I was already scheduled to make a mission trip back to Brazil, to a region of the country that I had not seen in twenty years. On the last night, the thought hit me: 'Why not bring this to Brazil?'

Todd had made it very clear that the revival was 'nameless and faceless.' Even so, I asked if he was okay with me taking the revival to Brazil. His response was the same, "Of course you can!"

The very next day, Pastor Mervin Strother called me and said, "I believe God told me to go to Brazil with you."

We ended up buying a ten-foot inflatable swimming pool, and we were off to Brazil to hold revival meetings in four different cities through water baptism, believing that Jesus would meet the people in the water and baptize them in the Holy Ghost and fire!

The thought did cross my mind a couple of times, "What if people think you are nuts? What if nobody wants to be baptized again?"

Then, of course, there was always the mocking voice saying, "A Wal-Mart swimming pool? Cold water? This ain't Kansas, Honey."

Well, it turned out to be one of the most awesome weeks of ministry in my life. We baptized well over a thousand people in those four nights. Literally hundreds were filled with the Holy Spirit for the first time, speaking in other tongues.

Weeping and wailing in repentance was the norm! There was such deep repentance that we created the concept of a wailing wall. As people came out of the pool they would make their way to a nearby wall in the church and stay there crying out to God in heart-felt repentance. No rushing off to change clothes! Dripping wet, they just cried out to Heaven!

One night, we baptized until 4:00 in the morning. I was exhausted, but the line seemed as if it would never end.

Donnie Shaffer, Central Church, Central, LA

# # # #

BIBLIOGRAPHY

Books

Campbell, Duncan, *Revival in the Hebrides*, Krause House, 2016

Welchel, Tommy & Griffith, Michelle P., *True Stories of the Miracles of Azusa Street and Beyond,* Shippensburg, PA, Destiny Image Publishers, 2013

Cheetham, J. Keith, *On the Trail of John Wesley*, Edinburgh, UK, Luath Press, 2003

Dallimore, Arnold, *George Whitefield: The Life and Times of the Great Evangelist of the Eighteenth-Century Revival*, Carlisle, PA, Banner of Truth, 1970

Articles

Trump and the Hebrides Revival

https://ndpwy.wordpress.com/2017/09/03/donald-trumps-connection-to-the-hebrides-revival/

Fulton Street Revival

https://patch.com/virginia/herndon/bp--fulton-street-noontime-prayer-and-revival-of-1857-58

Revival

https://www.charismanews.com/opinion/70114-history-proves-that-praying-for-revival-matters

Made in the USA
San Bernardino, CA
15 July 2020